BULLYING: A COMMUNITY APPROACH

To Mary,
Mark, Louise and Emily

Brendan Byrne

Bullying:
A
Community
Approach

the columba press

First published in 1994 by
the columba press
93 The Rise, Mount Merrion, Blackrock, Co Dublin
Reprinted 1996

Cover by Bill Bolger
Origination by The Columba Press
Printed in Ireland by Colour Books, Ltd, Dublin

ISBN 1 85607 103 0

Acknowledgements

Many people have made this book possible. However, I wish to single out for special mention my wife Mary for her untiring support and interest, and all the teachers, students and other adults with whom I have been in contact over the years. Sincere thanks to Derek Davis for permission to include his account on pages 25-27, which was first broadcast on the BBC Radio Ulster programme, *Sound Education*, in autumn 1993, and to Paul Bruton for permission to print the story on pages 43-45. I wish to express thanks also for permission to include the rap which introduces the section on drama on page 71. It opens a play on bullying by students from seventeen schools from within the area covered by the Southern Education and Library Board in Northern Ireland.

In the course of the book, names, personal and family details have been changed to ensure confidentiality.

Contents

Introduction   7

PART I: What they say about ...
Bullying   10
The Victim   11
The Bully   12
Being Bullied   13
The Silent Majority   15
The Effects of Bullying   15
The 'In' Group   16

PART II: The Background to Bullying
Bullying – What is it?   18
What makes a person a victim or a bully?   20
Bullying in the Workplace   28
Neighbourhood Bullying   31
Bullying in a youth setting   32
Bullying and Sports Clubs   34
The School Bus   35
Initiation Rites   37
Why victims don't tell   38
Conspiracy of Silence   41
The Long-Term Effects of Bullying   42

PART III: Responses to Bullying

Developments in various countries   50

What parents can do   60

A Community Approach to Bullying   65

Helping Bullies   80

The Theory in Practice   81

Conclusion   82

Resources   85

Contacts   90

Index   94

Introduction

I have been a teacher since 1973. I had not been teaching very long, when I began to realise that certain people are subjected to very negative treatment from time to time. As a teacher, you get glimpses of it – crossing the yard, walking down a corridor or even in class. It is usually very subtle – a look, a gesture, a name. Bullying is difficult to detect. It is surrounded by a conspiracy of silence and often the person who least wants to speak out is the person being bullied.

Between 1985 and 1992, I carried out research at primary and post-primary schools to confirm my suspicion that bullying is a problem in schools. In February 1993, my book, *Coping with Bullying in Schools,* appeared. It generated a lot of media and public interest. In March, the Minister for Education, Ms Niamh Bhreathnach announced the setting up of a working group to draw up guidelines for countering bullying behaviour in primary and post primary schools. These were published in September 1993.

Until recently, bullying was considered to be exclusive to schools. This is not the case. Bullying can occur wherever people are in contact, in either small or large groups. Consequently, there have been reports of serious bullying not only in schools but in family units, in various work situations and in local neighbourhoods. The present book attempts to place bullying in the context of the wider community. The majority of children go to school and therefore schools are in a special position to raise the awareness of bullying behaviour and the devastating effect it can have on a person, both in the school and long-term. However, the responsibility goes beyond the schools. Bullying is a learned behaviour, most often from parents, brothers and sisters and the peer group. The behaviour is either reinforced or challenged by the atmosphere which exists in individual schools, workplaces and clubs. In my opinion, much greater emphasis should be put on preventative measures.

Over the last number of years I have spoken to large numbers of parents, teachers, pupils and youth leaders. I have had contact with people who work with young offenders. Adults who have been bullied have also contacted me. This book is based on the stories of many people. It considers what is happening in other countries and attempts to dispel the myth that the current interest in bullying is just a fad.

Raising awareness of what bullying is and of its consequences is the most effective way of encouraging people to do something about it. Bullying is a form of anti-social behaviour which is based on an abuse of power. We have a choice. In the words of Michele Elliott, director of the children's charity, Kidscape:

> 'You have to decide what kind of society you want to have; dog eat dog or something more humane and constructive'.

Brendan Byrne
19 August, 1994

PART I

What they say about …

Bullying

'As a former teacher, I have always been conscious of the incidence of bullying and its effect on young people. I know that childhood bullying can cause severe damage – in some cases having a permanent effect on the victim's life right into his or her adulthood. I believe that every pupil has the basic right to physical and psychological safety and well-being in school.'

Niamh Bhreathnach
Minister For Education, Dublin

'While one will find people who will say they were bullied, I think you'll find very few who will admit to bullying themselves. I see it as one end of a spectrum which extends into marriage, family relationships, business and so on, the intimidation of those who are that little bit different, weak or vulnerable, and not something which stops at Leaving Cert. It's that horrible seduction of the group, while – it's very sad – some people seem to be nature's victims.'

Dr Anthony Clare

'We mess a lot in our class, hitting and pushing. I always join in but there are one or two new boys who I find extremely annoying and when we're messing I try to hit them the most and the hardest.'

13 year old boy

'Bullying is slow, painful torture.'

14 year old girl

'We used to pick on her and say 'dumb-head Joan'. We'd brush against her and say "Yuk, we've got Joan's germs now." She had no friends and got so upset. It got so bad she didn't want to come to school. I feel very bad about what we did. We're friends with her now.'

14 year old girl

'Bullying nowadays is a way of life. I have been called names because of how I looked. I used to think "why me?" I thought there was something wrong with me. I just live with the idea of being called names.'

16 year old girl

The Victim

'She was slagged about her parents. They're separated. She skipped most of second year. She wouldn't go back to school. She even hurt herself so they wouldn't send her back. She's getting counselling now.'

15 year old girl about classmate

'I feel that people that are bullied are usually quiet and not very noticeable. They never make themselves heard. In this way they won't say much if they are being pushed around and bullied. They usually aren't part of a large group of friends and find it hard to mix.'

14 year old girl

'This subject has been on my mind for years. It fills me with grief and misery to think what weak and nervous children go through at school – how their health and character for life are destroyed by rough and brutal treatment.'

Letter in the preface to the sixth edition of
Tom Brown's Schooldays *by Thomas Hughes, (1857).*

'I noticed a certain fellow in second or third year who was sort of weird looking. He was always nervous and sticking to himself, so much so when somebody said something to him he would run off. I noticed a smaller boy hitting him hard over the head with a heavy book, repeatedly, and the fellow wasn't doing anything. I saw even the sixth years laughing at him. Once I had to restrain myself from slagging him.'

16 year old boy

'I was warned to stay away from the "space creature". I'm sure that there isn't a boy in my class who isn't ashamed of what happened to P. Any property he had was regarded as useless or diseased. People used to pay football with his stereo, after all it was only P's. He never had any money to buy clothes, so we called him "smelly knacker". In class he was constantly slagged because he wasn't particularly bright. We took turns beating him up.'

16 year old boy

The Bully

'He picked on me not because of the way I looked or anything, just because he didn't like me.'

13 year old boy

'The bully is a highly strategic person. Using his tactical methods he is able to locate the victim's Achilles heel and hammer home on this. In the case of mental bullying, the bully lowers the self-esteem of the victim, and that makes him feel worthless. Speaking from personal experience, even if the bullying stops, the victim still carries the mark. He is extremely self–aware, self–critical. This ultimately leads to total depression and possible suicide.'

17 year old boy

'He was a small chubby boy with brown hair. He was the sort of boy everyone was afraid of and if he dropped his coat someone would pick it up and give it to him. He was a sore loser and a bully and if you did something out of line he would be after you. He was really tough and once said he was the strongest in the school. He was probably one of the weakest in the class.'

14 year old girl

'I'm scared of him,' said Piggy, 'and that's why I know him. If you're scared of someone you hate him but you can't stop thinking about him. You kid yourself he's all right really, an' then when you see him again; it's like asthma an' you can't breathe.'

Piggy talking about Jack in
Lord of the Flies *by William Golding.*

Being Bullied

'Forty–four years ago, I was bullied and I still remember it as the only thing that ever made me want to commit murder. It went on for several weeks and involved arm-twisting and so on, but I remember the constant fear. It stayed with me until a few years ago, to the point that I felt like going back and shooting the guy, which in a way I dealt with in *Too Late For Logic*. Schoolyard bullies are torturers – you can't reason with them, and even the victim gets pulled into that unreason.'

Tom Murphy (Playwright)

'I have big ears and I'm fattish. My dad doesn't have a brilliant job. I was slagged about everything. I'm the kind of person who takes everything in. Everything bad someone says about me, I change it as soon as possible. Now I've lost that weight but I still have big ears and my dad's job is still the same.'

14 year old girl

'When I get dressed in the morning or at night, I make sure nobody is around because I'm ashamed of my size and being fat. But that is just so I won't get slagged any more. I cannot handle the slagging at the moment. If it got any worse, I wouldn't be able to handle it.'

15 year old boy

'I was bullied for four years. I used to be called "shit" because I had very dark skin. I changed school but I was still bullied. They even got a rumour sent around that I was beaten at home. That really hurt.'

15 year old boy

'I dreaded the morning. I was dying. I didn't want to go to school. I wanted to be dead.'

13 year old girl

'I was the new girl. I went to a mixed school. People would run off on me and talk, laugh about me. I was sent disgusting notes and cards. The experience was the worst thing of my life.'

15 year old girl

'The worst part of bullying is the loneliness.'

15 year old girl

'Pain is not the worst thing in bullying. It's the fear, fear of meeting the bully again.'

14 year old boy

'It feels sad and painful to be called these names and when people who you thought were your friends consistently slag you and make up slags for you, it's very painful and hurtful. You feel alone and hated.'

14 year old girl

'I get slagged because I'm slightly overweight. It can soon begin to hurt if you are called "Fatso", "Fatty", or "Chubby", day in day out. It's just a strong tradition in schools – slagging.'

16 year old boy

The Silent Majority

'A solution to bullying can only be found by the year itself. Others should have the moral courage to stand up to the ringleader.'

18 year old boy

'Nobody likes or wants bullies around but very seldom is the time when someone plucks up enough courage to tell the bullies to stop.'

15 year old boy

The Effects of Bullying

'He has been isolated since the beginning of First Year and even now, in Sixth Year, he has not been accepted. It is on and off but it will never stop. He himself has hardened, gone into himself. Even when you try to be civil now, he thinks that you are just "taking the piss". I don't think that he will recover from what we did to him. Personally I have nothing against him. I slag him now because of his resentful personality which I suppose he mostly developed because of the treatment he received.'

18 year old boy

'A friend of mine was being constantly called "pufter" and "queer" day in day out by the whole class. It eventually got to the stage that he believed them. When he told me he thought he was gay he asked me if I thought he was. It took him ages before he had more confidence in himself but he's alright now. Basically what I'm saying is if you hear something enough you start to believe it!'

15 year old boy

The bully does not realise how much he/she can ruin somebody's confidence. I was a victim and even now I find it hard to get all my courage together to join a group that are chatting.'

18 year old girl

'He was slagged about his sight since First Year. It got more serious. He became paranoid and extremely untrusting of anyone. I tried many times to talk to him and establish a link but constantly he thinks I'm attacking him. I see this person for a long time not connecting with people or trusting other people.'

18 year old boy

'Although I'm fairly popular and respected now, I still suffer insecurity from time to time, even depression, even though it was nine years ago.'

18 year old boy

The 'In' Group

'There is always a core group around which the bullying starts. Inside that group two or three can lead the herd. Usually the followers don't want to bully but these two or three do, so they are forced into the attack. The core group think they are above the rest. They hold all the power, so they think. I think whenever they feel this power being threatened they up the slagging to regain their supremacy.'

14 year old girl

'I was bullied myself when I came from America to Ireland at the age of twelve. All the girls of the class whom I really looked up to and liked, sat at a table together. They and the boys teased me and called me names. They made me feel out of their group. But I was small and weak and the youngest.'

14 year old girl

PART II

The Background to Bullying

Bullying – What is it?

It is difficult to get an agreed definition of what constitutes bullying behaviour, or of a bully and a victim. An examination of a bullying incident will often focus on whether it is physical or mental, or a combination of both. While the common view of bullying is that it is usually physical, the reality is different. Most bullying takes the form of slagging, jeering, name-calling, teasing and the deliberate provocation of the victim. In some cases rumours are started. This is especially common among girls, where comments are made about a person's sexual behaviour. Terms such as 'slut' and 'slag' are commonly used. Slagging is a wide-ranging word that can be used to describe everything from comments about physical appearance and clothes to comments about sexual orientation. At the level of harmless banter, a person's hair-cut could be the focus of attention. Much more hurtful and damaging could be comments about a person's physical appearance, e.g. big ears, a big nose, small or large size. Boys in particular engage in two very upsetting forms of slagging. The first is where a person is called queer, bent or gay. This can start very simply. Perhaps there is a boy in second year in secondary school whose voice hasn't broken. Maybe a boy looks somewhat effeminate or isn't very skillful at the sport played by the majority of the boys. Somebody calls him 'Rosie' or 'Sheila'. He is seen to become very upset. This becomes a source of fun, so the name sticks. Imagine the effect if this persists for one or two years or even longer.

The second form of slagging common particularly among boys is where comments are made about a person's mother, sister or girlfriend, often with a sexual innuendo. This is one of the most common causes of physical fights among boys.

Another difficulty in defining this behaviour relates to deciding at what point certain behaviour becomes bullying. It is accepted that among young people there is a lot of slagging, name-calling and physical contact (horseplay). This is perfectly normal. It becomes bullying when the same person or persons are repeatedly on the receiving end of negative attention, against their wishes, but they are unable to stop it.

The question of how long the behaviour is going on provides a third difficulty. The term bullying should not include the isolated incident. Rather, it should refer to a longer period of time – weeks, months and even years. In some of the really severe cases of bullying I have dealt with, I have spoken to people who have been bullied for six or seven years.

In reaching definitions, one must ask of the person bullying, 'Do they do it deliberately?' My experience suggests that there is a small number of bullies who know exactly what they are doing and actually enjoy inflicting pain and suffering on their victim. They usually get a 'buzz' out of what they do. However there are many people who get involved in bullying behaviour, especially as part of a group, and they are unaware of the suffering that they are causing.

I am reminded of a situation where a boy in fourth class in primary school had been jeered in the yard because he always wore a big woolly scarf. 'They spread the word that I was a "Mammy's boy". They put me in the corner, and everyone crushed me by piling in on top of me. They always said, "We're going to put you in the squashy corner".' When he eventually told his mother what was happening, he concluded by saying, 'Mam, it's normal for me, it's part of my everyday life.' When the class was confronted with what they were doing the common excuse was, 'But we only did it for a laugh, we never meant any harm by it.' This was probably true for the majority, but in cases such as this there is usually a ringleader, the real bully, who orchestrates the behaviour and who has the power to get the others to join in.

The numbers involved in bullying vary. Sometimes it can just be one person bullying another. Then again it can be two, three, four, right up to a situation where the whole group turns on an individual. This is devastating for the victim where everybody slags them and nobody will include them or support them. Some definitions of bullying contend that to be called bullying there must be a wilful, conscious desire to hurt somebody else. In my opinion, where a group is involved in bullying there is nearly always a person who has this motive, but the rest of the group should not be exonerated.

With these constraints in mind, I feel the most appropriate definitions, in the school context, are the following:

Bully: A boy or girl who fairly often oppresses or harasses somebody else. The target may be boys or girls, the harassment physical or mental.

Victim: A boy or girl who for a fairly long time has been and still is exposed to aggression from others – that is boys or girls from his or her own class, or maybe from other classes, pick fights and are rough with him or her or tease and ridicule him or her. (Olweus, 1978, 34-35)

Bullying is repeated aggression, verbal, psychological or physical, conducted by an individual or group against others. (*Guidelines on Countering Bullying Behaviour in Primary and Post Primary Schools*, 1993, 6)

What makes a person a victim or a bully?

'The is always someone who gets the hard time, and sometimes you don't even need a ringleader.'   15 year old boy

At the outset, it must be said that there is no typical bully or victim. In addition, it is unlikely that a single factor is significant. Rather it is the combination of factors which is most important. It may be useful to speak of risk factors. The following could be seen as risk factors:

1. Physical characteristics.
2. Personality traits.
3. Family background.
4. Changes in family circumstances.
5. Jealousy.
6. Atmosphere in school/club/workplace.

The stereotype view of a person who is bullied is often that of the fat person, the slim person, the very tall or the very short person, the person with a big nose or big ears, red hair or glasses. The stereotype often includes people with speech irregularities, for example, the person who has a stutter or stammer, the person with a high-pitched, squeaky voice or who mumbles so that others have difficulty in hearing what they are saying. However, this stereotype is far too simplistic, because we know that not all people with the characteristics mentioned are bullied. Therefore, it must be something more.

I believe that the personality type which puts a person most at risk is the shy, sensitive type where the person tends to take everything to heart and personalises any negative comments. Consider the child who gets a new coat, or even a hair cut, and on going to school the next day finds that somebody makes a smart comment. They come home in the evening and stand in front of the mirror wondering, 'Do I really look as bad as they say?' Often they refuse to believe their parents who tell them that not everybody is trying to make fun of them and hurt them. It is important that a child learns to distinguish between the kind of comment that everybody is subjected to from time to time and the comment deliberately intended to hurt. Over-reaction by sensitive children is exactly what a bully wants.

Some parents may unwittingly over-protect their children and in the longer term make them more vulnerable. These parents have a very pure motive – they want the best for their children – but sometimes it prevents the children developing a sense of independence.

The atmosphere in a school or club will either support bullying behaviour or lead to its reduction. Consider a school or club which allows its pupils or members to be aggressive towards one another either physically or verbally, e.g. to push, shove, kick, or make fun of somebody who is different in either appearance or personality or background. This leads to an atmosphere which is conducive to bullying behaviour. If, on the other hand, the school or club has drawn up an anti–bullying code, has a policy for dealing with the behaviour and maybe has an anti–bullying week each year, that school or club is doing a lot to create a supportive, caring atmosphere where bullying is far less likely to take place.

In my experience the words which other young people use most often to describe those who are bullied are:

  Different
  Quiet
  Don't retaliate

The fact that most victims do not retaliate is seen by many as the kernel of the problem. The implication is that it is almost their own fault that they are being picked on. I reject this and put the problem firmly on the side of the person bullying. I will return to this point later.

It is possible to speak about a provocative victim, that is a person who seems to bring a lot of negative attention on him or herself by being excessively attention seeking, for example by persistently getting into trouble deliberately. Sometimes trying too hard to get into a certain group may be the source of the problem.

Those who are perceived as different attract certain scrutiny from people in general, but the bully in particular. This perceived difference can refer to appearance, personality or background. Also certain hobbies or interests (opera, ballet, train spotting) can sometimes trigger negative comments, especially where males are concerned.

It is now generally accepted that bullying is a *learned* behaviour. This behaviour is modelled most of all on that of parents, older brothers and sisters. If aggression, either physical or verbal, is the norm at home, that behaviour is likely to be modelled. It is my belief that the impact of verbal aggression is often underestimated. I am thinking of parents who say things to their children like 'you're stupid', 'you're a nuisance', 'all you ever do is cause us trouble'. Children receiving those negative messages don't feel good about themselves. Consequently they may displace these feelings by bullying somebody weaker and more vulnerable than they are. There has been quite an amount of debate among researchers into bullying behaviour as to whether or not bullies have lower self-esteem than people who do not bully. It is important to say that some bullies will have low self-esteem and others high, but my own findings would indicate that victims have the lowest self-esteem, followed by the bullies.

In discussing why some people bully, there is a danger that a difficult home background will always be used to explain the behaviour. In my experience, most people who bully do have difficult home backgrounds, but there are some who do not. Some people who bully are nasty individuals who have a predisposition to aggressive behaviour. Among younger children, it is quite common to find that spoiled children bully others. It is normal for these children to get their own way. They are most often seen in pre-school play groups and in junior infant classes in primary school. Even at this young age the behaviour needs to be unlearned.

Jealousy is one of the main causes of bullying. The generally accepted idea that the victim of bullying is always different in some way is too simplistic. Coming in contact with a person who does not like you, or who is jealous of you, could lead to victimisation, if that person has the influence to control and manipulate a group so that they turn against you. It is often a case of being in the wrong place at the wrong time. If you had been in a different class or a different school, it would probably never have happened. An example of this is where a particular pupil is bright, conscientious and making excellent progress. If there are pupils who are threatened by this, or who feel jealous, the pupil may become known as a 'swot', 'lick' or 'teacher's pet'. This is not usually done overtly but rather by a series of whispers, glances, graffiti, and even licking noises. A case such as this presents particular difficulties for a teacher.

Changes in family circumstances, like unemployment, separation of parents, birth of a new baby, may cause a person to become a temporary bully or victim. In most cases this is just a passing stage, but without intervention it can become long-term.

Finally, a major complication in dealing with bullying behaviour is that people can be both bully and victim, depending on the circumstances – the so called 'bully victim'. For example, a person may be bullied at school and then displace feelings of anger and frustration onto a younger brother or sister at home.

Over the years I have interviewed many young people on the issue of bullying behaviour. In relation to physique, two questions I asked were:

Are bullies always bigger and stronger?
Do bullies always hit?

A summary of the answers to the first question would suggest that if you were a boy up to the age of about nine or ten, then bullies were often bigger and stronger. However, the majority of girls and older boys suggested that it was not so much the physical size of the bully that mattered, but rather the body language. Shoulders and fists were held high, and the voice was often used as a weapon to intimidate others. A remarkable number of people referred to the way the bully looks at you. This 'look' was associated with intimidation and had the ability to induce fear. It is interesting to note that quite often the bullies are actually quite small, but have the ability to project themselves as 'big' people, almost larger than life figures.

The consensus was that most bullies do not hit. However, they are very adept at letting the victim know that, if they have to, they will.

Television personality Derek Davis seems an unlikely target, but there were times the bullies pushed him to the brink of a nervous breakdown. This is how he told his story:

> 'When people see my physical size, they say 'how was a lad like that ever bullied?' They forget that somebody who may be 6' 2" and umpteen stone now, was once maybe four foot something and still fat, and I think that the typical bully's victim is always perhaps a wee bit different – the child who is fat, or the child who is spotty, the child who is skinny, but they are different. I was overweight. I was a very fat child and you know children will identify that and once, of course, your Achilles heel is identified, once that someone knows they can get to you by calling you 'fatso' or 'fatty' or whatever, then they will do it, and children can be, as everybody knows, very cruel and very uncaring. Very often the bullies are interesting. The bullies that I remember were quite small. Now they could be stocky and could be quite tough and aggressive or whatever, but they weren't the cool clean-cut sporting heroes – they were inadequate personalities or inadequate physiques themselves who were covering up that by targeting somebody who was more vulnerable and by directing the attention of a class or a group towards them.

> There was a degree of violence. Again you see, I had been gently reared. I was bigger than most of my contemporaries. My mother, who was obviously a big influence on me, absolutely forbade me to retaliate physi-

cally to anybody, any school child, in case I'd hurt them for God's sake! Now it didn't take the pint-sized bullies too long to twig that they could run up and hit me a dig and I wouldn't retaliate because the mammy had instructed me not to, with the result that, yes, within a short time I was collecting more than the occasional dig.

You accepted it as a certain norm. My mother was a Roman Catholic from the South of Ireland. My father, a good Northern, Ulster Unionist, Protestant from East Belfast. Now, one would have thought that that's grand, that establishes one well in both camps, so that gives you a great pedigree. Unfortunately, in childhood it meant that you were never accepted as a real Prod when I was at Protestant school and perhaps not even as a real Catholic, in the Catholic school, because of the cultural differences as much as the religious differences. In my case there was the physical difference, but there was also the religious and cultural differences as well.

I think that the bullying definitely stopped when I was probably coming up to my final year in school. My early years were unalloyed misery. I don't remember any childhood suicides or anything else like that but I can remember being in the deepest despair and almost, believe it or not, almost becoming anorexic at one point as a result of it, retreating into myself, not wanting to be the butt of jokes or physical abuse at mealtimes. It was wretched.

You feel useless and inadequate and if somebody keeps calling you a fat, useless lump, then that reinforces a very poor self-image and, yes, I did have a poor self-image and there was a point I remember, somewhere in my middle teens, you know the way, if you're coping with puberty and you're trying to chat up girls, and you're coping with blackheads and spots and pimples and obesity and all the rest of it, and you have such a rotten self-image that you become absolutely desperate.

There was a point where I was embarrassed to walk into a room. It was only in my first year in University that I would take my jacket off in a discotheque or at a function, I was that physically shy and all of that, because of that rotten self-image.'

That account highlights the following points about bullying behaviour:

* Derek was obviously different because of his weight. Probably more important than the difference was the fact that the bullies had found his Achilles heel. Being fat was probably the trigger for the bullying behaviour

* The bullies that he remembers were quite small. What seems to be most important is the positive attitude to aggression.

* The bullies displaced their own feelings of inadequacy onto somebody more vulnerable than they were.

* His mother's instruction not to retaliate may have run counter to a natural inclination to hit back if provoked. The attitude in schools at that time, to telling somebody you were being bullied, would have been very negative. Hence, the fact that he accepted it as the norm.

* While he doesn't remember any childhood suicides, he paints a bleak picture of his early years in school – 'unalloyed misery', 'deepest despair', 'wretched'. Most researchers have suggested that bullying decreases as students move up the school. This should not deflect attention from the fact that very serious bullying can persist right up to the final years of school.

* Like most people being bullied, Derek retreated into himself.

* Damage to self–image is one of the worst effects of bullying – 'You feel useless and inadequate'.

Bullying in the Workplace

It is remarkable that, for so long, bullying was considered to happen only in schools. In 1992, Andrea Adams, a freelance broadcaster and journalist, wrote a book entitled *Bullying at Work,* as a result of public response to her two BBC Radio 4 documentaries on bullying, 'An Abuse of Power' and 'Whose fault is it anyway?' The book has generated huge debate on the issue. In the Spring of this year, BBC television produced a programme with the same title as the book, with Adams as consultant.

Andrea Adams contends that bullying at work is beginning to be recognised as a significant factor contributing to workplace stress. It literally makes a person ill. This illness may take the form of minor aches and pains, severe headaches, stomach and bowel problems. There are also emotional effects – anxiety, anger, loss of confidence, feelings of isolation and reduced self-esteem. Bullying causes mental ill-health in the workplace.

This view is echoed by Dr Heinz Legman, a Swedish expert in this field. He described bullying as a form of psychological terrorisation. The victim experiences trauma which causes stress disorder which may eventually lead to chronic illness in the form of depression and/or obsession. Professor Carey Cooper, of the University of Manchester Institute of Science and Technology, has studied stress in the workplace and the factors that cause it. He estimates that one third to half of all stress-related illnesses are due to bullying. As well as damage to the victim, bullying at work also causes stress-related absenteeism, with consequent loss of productivity and profits.

A survey of bullying in the workplace by Staffordshire University, reported in the BBC programme, found that 53% had witnessed bullying. Only 19% said that they were the only ones bullied, suggesting that most bullies have several victims. The bullies were most often either line managers (41%) or senior line managers (30%). The most common triggers of bullying were the victim changing job or the appointment of a new manager. The survey also found that 27% of people left their employment as a result of bullying. The victims used the following descriptions of bullying: intimidation, verbal abuse on a daily basis and regular public humiliation.

If a person is bullied at work, Adams advises that he or she keep a written account of what has been happening and approach the personnel department and Trade Union. In a small number of companies, employees have access to employee assistance programmes. Where victims have lost a job because of bullying, they have the option to take the case to an Industrial Tribunal, but this involves considerable personal expenditure. A survey of the top one hundred companies in Britain, also carried out by the BBC programme, showed that 25% of companies were of the opinion that bullying was not a problem and 67% of companies said that there were 'no cases' in their organisation.

In Sweden, Dr Legman has a clinic to help victims of workplace bullying. The course lasts for four weeks and costs £5,000stg. It is paid for by the state insurance company and the employer, who under Swedish law has a legal responsibility in this situation to pay part of the costs. The thinking behind this approach is that the effects of bullying at work represent a high cost to society.

There has been no research into bullying at work in an Irish context. Simon's story indicates that there is a very urgent need to study this phenomenon in Ireland. Simon is twenty-seven years old and worked in the accounts section of a large company:

> There were five men working in our section with an overall boss. The boss we had for the previous six months had to go on sick leave. The person who replaced him wasn't really there very much. Within a few days, two of the fellows were inclined to be domineering, wanting to have a say in everything, wanting to

run the office really. They were basically nice fellows, but as time passed they became more and more opinionated and outspoken. One of them, Sean, seemed to take on the role of substitute boss. He took to commenting on my work, belittling my efforts, with comments like 'you're stupid and incompetent'. In any kind of discussion I got things like, 'That's stupid, what would you know about that?' These incidents began to happen regularly, up to two or three times a day. Sean's friend Liam often tried to get a cheap laugh at my expense by making comments about my appearance. Presumably he would soon have forgotten those comments, but I didn't. What made it even worse was that, if anyone from outside came into our section, Sean and Liam were all smiles and pleasant – even to me. The two others in the office never commented on what was happening, one way or the other. Within two months, I was distressed and preoccupied. The whole situation had affected my ability to work. After six months I decided to ask for a transfer to another section.

It takes great courage for a person in a situation like this to report what is going on. Because so few companies have a policy on bullying at work there is a danger of being viewed as a troublemaker or 'crank'. The person may not be supported by colleagues and may end up very much alone. This is probably the reason why so many people affected in this way find it easier to request a transfer to a different section or even seek a new job. In the present economic climate this is a major infringement of their rights.

Neighbourhood Bullying

Neighbourhood bullying can be very difficult to deal with, because of the inclination most people have to avoid confrontation if at all possible, especially where neighbours are involved. Most people hope that the problem is not really serious and that it will pass. If it is real bullying, it tends not to go away.

In its most extreme form, a whole community may be intimidated. This can happen where certain members of the community are involved in criminal activity. However, it is more common for an individual family or a member of a family to be singled out. I am reminded of a situation in rural Ireland, where a dispute arose between two families over a right of way. One farmer approached the difficulty in a very reasoned, polite manner and suggested that the matter be resolved with the help of a solicitor. Eventually, it was decided that he was in the right and that seemed to be the end of the matter. However, it was really only the beginning, because the two adults and the four children of the other family embarked on a campaign of intimidation and vilification which lasted for two years and was only ended by the intervention of the police. The campaign took the form of public verbal abuse (especially in school by the children), abusive telephone calls, rumour mongering, graffiti and physical intimidation.

Jealousy can sometimes be the motive for bullying in a neighbourhood. A particular family may begin to enjoy greater material success than their neighbours as evidenced by a new car, new windows etc. Members of minority groups, religious or ethnic, may also be singled out. Children may also be subjected to bullying, sometimes at a very early age. Sadly it is often the shy, sensitive child who is picked out. Maybe they cry easily, or find it hard to make friends. Just as in workplace bullying, the neighbourhood bully usually has more than one victim. This is why there is such scope for co-operation between adults on a street or in an area in order to counter the behaviour.

The following story, told by a mother, shows the anxiety and suffering which can result from neighbourhood bullying:

They changed towards her once she went to a different secondary school. The worst part was the name-calling. They would group together and if she came home from the shops or was late from school the abuse would start in front of everybody. Then they started making phone-calls, shouting obscene comments and making horrible noises. Sometimes they would pretend to invite her to a slumber party, then laugh and jeer down the phone. At the beginning she pretended not to hear them but she eventually stopped going out. Even the girls who used to be friendly with her stayed away. It was heartbreaking. I can't describe the anguish we all felt as a family. It was so hard to know what to do. What made the situation really difficult was the way this group of girls were so nice to everybody on the road – going out of their way to be friendly and obliging. I tried bringing up the subject with one or two mothers but they didn't want to get involved. I can understand that now I suppose. They had no quarrel with these young people. They probably thought I was imagining things. We moved house. It was the only thing we could do to stop the nightmare.

Neighbourhood bullying needs to be confronted by as many members of a community as possible. This requires courage, commitment and an interest in the welfare of others.

Bullying in a youth setting

There are many opportunities for young people to come together as a formal group – youth clubs, scouts, girl guides, community projects and sports clubs. Bullying in a youth setting is often exacerbated by the broad age-range that many youth clubs and projects cater for. A 'pecking order' can develop, i.e. the older youths bully the younger ones. The key person in raising awareness of bullying behaviour and its effects is the person with overall authority, because he or she is in a position to set standards on the issue. For example if the leader says 'Bullying? We don't have that problem in our club,' it is very difficult for other people working in that situation to create an atmosphere where bullying is less likely to occur. If, on the other hand, the leader adopts the approach that there is probably a certain amount of bullying behaviour wherever people come together in groups, the people in charge can then decide what steps to take in order to prevent or at least reduce the incidence of bullying. All people working in a youth setting need to discuss formally the issue of bullying and reach a consensus about what approach (if any) they wish to adopt.

Youth workers should make sure that people who are new to the club/project/centre are made feel welcome. A child or young person could be suffering in silence over quite a long period of time unless encouraged to speak out by an active anti–bullying policy.

Bullying tends to happen where there is a lack of adult supervision. As in school, initiation rites can be a problem. In general, toilets, corridors, and the immediate surrounds present opportunities for bullying. In addition, should the club be involved on an outing by coach, some people may be subjected to negative attention. All of this highlights the importance of adequate supervision. This is dependent on having sufficient youth workers available at all times. Many youth clubs operate a system of junior leaders, i.e. older members of the club with responsibility for looking after some of the younger members and their activities. If monitored carefully, this could be used to increase supervision levels, but the system itself is open to abuse and could actually increase bullying in some circumstances.

When bullying occurs, parents of the bully and the victim

should be notified. Should a situation arise where it is necessary to rescind club membership, the parents will have been forewarned. Partnership between parents and club or project leaders is very important.

Bullying and Sports Clubs

Like schools and youth clubs, sports clubs may have an atmosphere which either reduces bullying behaviour to a minimum or allows or even encourages situations where it may happen. In the vast majority of cases in this context, we are not talking about bullying as a systematic, repeated behaviour where the same individuals are singled out for negative treatment. Rather I refer to the creation of a climate where aggressive behaviour is the norm. Most often, it is represented by the general approach of those in charge, usually adults. This tends to be much more common in the case of team sports.

The following elements may be characteristic of this climate:

* An over-competitive approach – 'win at all costs'. There may be very little emphasis on taking part in the sport for fun or the social benefits.

* Over aggressive language is accepted as the norm. This would be evident in training but particularly on match days during the warm-up session (dressing rooms) and throughout the game. Major importance is attached to establishing physical and mental superiority over the opposition by means of intimidation.

* During the game, coaches/mentors may make critical or abusive comments about the opposition players, the referee and even their own players. Sometimes this becomes verbal abuse. It is particularly upsetting for a player to be publicly criticised and/or humiliated by their own coach.

Many coaches/mentors are excellent role models and represent all that is best in sport. However some, unconsciously in most cases, create an over–aggressive atmosphere. It is acknowledged that in team sports, particularly physical contact sports, it is necessary to motivate a team to a high degree and controlled aggression is part of that.

The following story illustrates what can happen:

> John was eleven years old and big for his age. He played for the school soccer team at full–back. Some of his friends were joining the local club soccer team so John did also. Pat, a middle aged, long-standing member of the club, was coach. At the first training session, John noticed that Pat shouted a lot and used bad language. So did a lot of the players. After two weeks, John was picked to play against a local club. There was a long history of rivalry between the clubs. Because of his size, John was to play at centre forward. He did not play well. Each time he made a mistake, he heard the hurtful comments from Pat on the sideline – 'Come on John, a big fellow like you should be able to do better'. This pattern continued at training and in games, but the criticism became stronger and more personal. Comments were made to other players about John. He lost interest and stopped going to the club. The issue was never discussed …

The School Bus

Every schoolday, thousands of children go to and from school on the school bus. For some pupils school buses are like moving prisons. In rural areas, children are collected at designated points. Some children spend a lot of time on these buses every morning and evening. In the cities and towns many schools have a large catchment area and use private coach companies to bring pupils to school. In both situations, the only adult usually present is the driver. The bus driver cannot possibly be aware of everything that goes on behind his or her back. Their job is to drive the bus safely.

It is further complicated because there are unwritten rules for bullying on the school bus. First, make sure that the victim sits near the back of the bus. This is usually accomplished by threats. Second, it is risky to bully a person on your own, so get a group to join in. Third, don't physically bully the person, because the driver just might see a fist while looking in the mirror or hear a cry. It is just as effective to slag the person repeatedly or spit on them. There is also scope to take books and homework copies and drop them selectively onto the road. In winter, some pupils find that their coats are taken and dragged under the seats to be walked on.

One might well wonder why pupils do not tell somebody about this awful ordeal. However, when you know that you must travel on the same bus the next day, the next week, the next month, it is a daunting prospect to disclose what is going on. There is always the stigma of being seen as a 'rat' and what if the information is badly handled by either the bus driver, parents or the school? For many pupils the risk is too great and so they prefer to suffer in silence.

It should be pointed out that bus drivers can also be the focus of attention from a bully gang. Present on the bus there is the silent majority, the ones who see bullying going on but who do nothing about it. They are not bullying or being picked on themselves but their silence allows it to happen.

There is need for far greater co-operation between schools, bus drivers, parents and pupils on the issue of bullying on school buses. The bus driver should not feel solely responsible for behaviour on the bus or feel blame for misbehaviour. With the numbers involved, they should be encouraged to report incidents and/or individuals to the school authorities. Parents should also report incidents to the school. Any investigation by the school should be carried out in a low key way.

Initiation Rites

'Some things seem fun, like tying up someone, gagging them and hanging them upside down from a tree.'

15 year old boy

'It was September 8th. Michael, a first year student, waited at the bus stop just 200 yards from the school gates. Dressed in full school uniform, he caught the eye of some older students seeking an opportunity to 'hop' a first year. They quickly surrounded him, and forced him down a side street, heading for waste ground nearby. Terrified and unable to defend himself anyway, he was held securely while the gang scattered his books, copies and pencil box around the waste area. Laughing and jeering at his terror, they then tied him to a post and left him convulsed and crying. Two hours later Michael was released by a man walking his dog ...'

Is this a boyish prank or a serious act of aggression? Michael refused to go to school for two weeks after the incident. When he finally identified the older boys to the principal, they said that they had never intended any harm in what they had done. When they were in first year older students used to pick on them. In this way, bullying behaviour is perpetuated. There are less extreme examples within schools every year – ducking people's heads in toilets or taking wheels from their bicycles.

Some would argue that this behaviour is not bullying because it is once off rather than repeated. However, I would argue that it is a form of institutionalised bullying, repeated year after year.

If a school permits this kind of behaviour each year, it is creating an atmosphere which is conducive to bullying behaviour. Consider a new student who copes very badly with the negative attention from the older students. He or she is subsequently much more vulnerable to bullying from within their own year or class group.

New club members may also experience certain introductory rites. I am not objecting to fun in either schools or clubs. However, it should be fun for everybody. Sometimes it all goes too far. Older students/members need to be aware of this.

Why victims don't tell

'They say I'm thick and stupid. When I'm upset I think about it. I just want it to stop, but I just don't know what to do.'

16 years boy

One of the earliest messages given to children is 'Don't tell tales.' There is good reason for this. If parents and teachers were to be approached every time there was a difference of opinion, life would become intolerable. In addition, children would not develop the skills to resolve conflict. However, when a child is being bullied, this advice can cause major problems. As they get older, the precept of 'don't tell' becomes deeply ingrained on the minds of children. The terms used to describe those who do tell are very descriptive and off–putting – 'rat', 'snitch', 'grass', 'wimp', 'weed', 'snake'. Nobody wants to be in this category.

If you are being bullied and you decide to tell someone, be it parent, teacher or friend, there is often the underlying fear that the information may be badly handled, leaving you worse off than before.

There is a deep sense of shame associated with being bullied. It starts with a feeling of 'I don't like what they are doing.' It then moves to 'I don't like what they are doing but there is nothing I can do about it'. The final stage is 'I don't like what they are doing, there is nothing I can do about it, but they're all doing it, so there must be something wrong with me. It's my fault.' If people call you either fat, stupid or swot for long enough, with sufficient vindictiveness, self-confidence is replaced by deep-seated shame. It should be noted that many parents of children who are being bullied also experience this sense of shame. They wonder why their child is being subjected to this treatment and look for answers in the way they have brought up their children.

The fear and the shame mean that children seldom come straight out and say that they are being bullied. They drop hints about someone taking their things or writing on their copies. Older children may refer to a 'bad atmosphere' in their class or, more commonly, may refuse to speak about school at all.

There may be other less obvious indicators that something is wrong – extreme mood changes, headaches, loss of appetite, loss of interest in homework, decline in academic performance. When questioned on any of these issues, denial or anger is the most usual response.

Adults, even within the same family, can give very conflicting advice to children about how to deal with bullying behaviour, especially physical bullying. For many fathers, the approach is simple, especially if they are talking to their sons – hit back. Without realising it, the father in this situation is giving two messages to his child. Firstly, 'this is your problem, don't look to me for help'. Secondly, there is an implication that if the child is unable to stand up for himself, then there is something wrong with him. Mothers tend to be much more accepting of the fact that some children are, by nature, quiet and passive and find it extremely difficult to retaliate, especially in a physical way. Consequently, there may be open disagreement between parents about how a child should respond. If a child is being bullied over a period of time, they will be far less likely to look to such parents for guidance.

In my opinion most people, when pushed beyond a certain point, retaliate naturally. However, there are some people who are incapable of this reaction. For these people to retaliate is to go against their nature. I remember coming across the case of a young boy in second class of a primary school who was being bullied in the yard every day. For six weeks his father told him to hit back. Eventually, he did. He had to be dragged from the other child having fractured his skull. Such was the build-up of anger and frustration and feelings of inadequacy, that when he started he was unable to stop.

It would have been a much better course of action if the parents had approached the school and explained what was happening in the yard. In that way, the child being bullied would not have felt that it was his problem to sort out. I will come later to more positive advice which he could have been given.

Sometimes, parents will discover that their child is being bullied as a result of information from another parent whose child has told them what is happening. This can be a very distressing experience and often comes as a shock. The reaction of the bullied child is often denial. If pushed, the child may end up saying 'Mam, if you go to that school, I will never speak to you again'. With the possible exception of very young children, parents really should respect such a wish. It is necessary to build up the child's confidence to the point where they will allow an approach to be made to the school.

The fears of children about an approach to the school may be justified, because some parents do it in a very public way. If classmates see a parent waiting outside the principal's or teacher's door, they will ask questions. It is much less threatening for the child if the approach to the school is by letter or telephone. Anonymity is preserved. A further advantage is that those engaged in bullying can be observed. Once more, it is a low key rather than a public approach.

Conspiracy of Silence

Bullying happens because it is allowed to happen. In many ways it is much easier to turn a blind eye rather than do something about it. Consider the following:

> I clearly remember once when I made an effort to hang around with a person who was getting a lot of stick and bullying. Everyone we passed made sly and hurtful remarks, not alone to him but to me as well. This disheartened me a lot, so I ended up saying to myself 'Listen, I don't deserve this, to get slagged.' So I decided to keep my distance in the future.

This was a brave attempt to help someone, but unfortunately peer pressure was too strong. The majority of people are not involved in bullying, either as perpetrator or victim. They are bystanders. Some, through fear, may collude in the process.

People will stand up against bullying when an atmosphere is created which supports them in doing so. Schools and clubs need to raise awareness among pupils of the effects of bullying. Too often the excuse is 'we were only messing' or 'we never knew she was getting so upset'. Bullying awareness days, class charters and anti-bullying codes are effective ways of creating an atmosphere where people will say no to bullying behaviour. Parents also need to encourage their children to question how certain people are treated in school. Teachers need the structure of a school policy on bullying so that there is a set procedure for investigation of incidents.

The silent majority is also to be found in the workplace, in class and in neighbourhoods. The experience of this girl could refer to a number of contexts:

> It is horrific to watch but yet no one would dare report it to a teacher, due to the so called 'silent code'. It also gets to a point where you just couldn't be bothered about the victim. It becomes an everyday thing. It is

usual. It would be a weird and unusual day if the victim was not attacked for that day. The thing that frightens me most is the way in which none of us has the guts or, indeed, intelligence to tell anyone, even though we can see the pain and suffering of the victim being tortured.'

The Long-Term Effects of Bullying

I had no heart for life and became a nobody. There were two major bullies who destroyed me. They rarely hit me but they slagged me about some physical appearance. They wrecked my life. Every time I feel depressed or angry, these two boys come into my mind. I want to destroy them as they did me. I'm in sixth year now. It is very hard to recover from something like this because all you feel is hatred.

18 year old boy

At the worst, bullying can lead to suicide. Towards the end of 1982, three young people committed suicide in Norway. The local social service concluded that victimisation by peers over a long period of time was the reason for their suicides.

One of the worst effects of bullying is that it robs the victim of self-confidence. It can affect children and adults. It can happen within the space of a few months but the effects can last for years. One of the most basic needs of children in school is to be accepted as part of the larger class group and then to be part of a smaller, more intimate group. However, if a child is bullied for long enough, he or she builds up a barrier to keep the bullies out but usually it keeps everybody else out as well. As time passes the child becomes more and more isolated. Occasionally somebody in the class feels sorry for the isolated person and approaches them to join in a game or activity. Often, the response is 'leave me alone'. By this time suspicion and lack of confidence make it too threatening to take the risk. It must be pointed out that there are some very independent children who prefer their own company and are very happy that way. However, these children are very much in the minority.

I was contacted by Paul, a successful academic who had experienced bullying when he was in fifth class in primary school. When he went to secondary school, he was not bullied in any way. He seemed to have forgotten about his experience until he was twenty six and at university, engaged in postgraduate work. He had been feeling somewhat depressed and went to a counsellor who over a period of time discovered the legacy of what Paul had experienced on his journeys home from school. As a result, his ability to trust others was severely damaged. He became suspicious and inward looking. Only as an adult could Paul articulate the suffering involved. He wrote this story:

> They're always waiting at the corner or outside the school, usually three or four. R is usually in charge. He's always there. I ignore them but they know I've seen them. They know, and I know, it's a long walk home.
>
> I examine every crack in the road on the way. They're behind me, you see, and its better not to look up. Better also to keep at the same speed, keep my arms by my side, my hands in my pockets.
>
> Somebody mutters something about red hair – giggles – sharp, cutting giggles. I don't react. I try to raise my head and look straight ahead but it doesn't work. The whole world seems to stare at me. It's easier to look down, better to look down. How many seconds in a year?
>
> That's occupied a few more paces. Somebody cycles past. It's one of the casuals, one of the gang who joins in the game now and then. R always sends somebody up behind me on a bike. Somebody who can match my speed, no matter how fast I run. But I never run.
>
> 'How many seconds in a year?' shouts R to the bike rider. The bike rider shrugs! 'Who cares?'
>
> R knows I know things like this. R knows everything

about me. He plays on my name. Imagine if your name started with P! A chorus of 'Pee - Pee - Pee' from the followers. R quietens them down – not a good idea to attract attention.

R says he remembers me crying as a baby. He can't – I'm older than him. (What's June 17 minus Feb 9? 128 days – there!) He couldn't remember. But when I told him this he laughed and so do the others. Better to have said nothing. Keep my head down and say nothing.

The bike rider is waiting. I pass him. As I do, he just grins at me, through me. My heart is pounding, every muscle ready for flight. The pencil I had been gripping tightly in my coat pocket, snaps in my sweaty hand. I lose a lot of pencils that way.

Once I pass the bike rider I relax slightly and casually pluck a leaf off a laurel bush. No, stupid! They'll notice.

True to form a voice pipes up. 'Let's pull a leaf off that bush.' (It's R). 'Yes, let's,' chorus the others.

Why did I do it, why, why? I have let them get the upper hand. Don't ever do anything that might make them notice you. That's L ahead of me. He doesn't see me. Why didn't he wait for me? They never bother me when I'm walking with somebody. I can't call out. I can't call his name. It'll sound silly, like a little squeak and they'll hear it. Too late anyway. R has noticed L and has despatched the bike rider who passes me and catches up with L and starts to chat. L would have talked to me first. He knows me better. Not content to follow me home they have now hijacked the only friendly face I saw on the way.

The last few houses on the road look like the most gorgeous and peaceful places to live in. What bliss if I lived there and was home now. No time to think of home, they're still behind me and the junction gets closer. Better be sure I don't have to stop too long on the kerb. I pace myself with an approaching gap in the traffic and get across without having to wait.

Home. Home is the only place to go. Throw off this coat. Fling this school bag in the corner. Lego, Lego I can build anything with Lego and then I can change it anyway I want. With the door shut nobody can watch me. It'll be just me. Just me!

How many inches to the sun?

Paul's story highlights some of the main features of the relationship between a bully and a victim:

* The feeling of powerlessness in the face of the bully and his gang.

* The terrifying feeling that the whole world is looking at him and that the bully knows everything about him.

* The control the bully has over the rest of the gang.

* The attempts to distract himself from all the awful reality of the situation – by solving mathematical problems.

* The resentment that the bully and his group have taken all friends away from him.

* The dreadful isolation but safety represented by his room and his Lego.

Stephen also got in touch with me to explain how the treatment he received at school had affected him. He is now thirty-one.

I had the ideal family background. While this had many advantages it also led me to expect the rest of the world to be like this. In a sense, I was unprepared for the bad things that happen to all of us from time to time. Because of my idealised view of the world, if something had happened to me, I felt in some way that I was bad and in some way deserved it. Between the age of five and nine I had a very good friend. Then he moved away. My grandmother, to whom I was very close, died that year. I withdrew into myself. I had always been sensitive. By the time I went into secondary school, I was insecure, nervous and fearful. I found it difficult to adjust to the new situation.

By second year I was being subjected to name calling with a mental or obscene connotation – 'weirdo', 'pansy', 'queer', 'mental'. I found it disturbing and distressing. I began to internalise and personalise these things. Over a period of time, my mind stopped working, just as if somebody had taken the power out of it. My energy went – physically, mentally, every way. My studies went down. I had no aspirations or inspirations for when I would leave school. I spent hours doing nothing. Because it happened in an all-boys school, I came to associate that cruelty with males in general.

Eventually, I became locked into a role. I was perceived as freakish, peculiar, queer. I began to play their game, to give them what they expected. I realised that I had a certain entertainment value, that I was liked in an idiosyncratic way. I did not know how to break out of this role so that I made myself into a parody of myself. I became self-conscious about being normal. Ironically, there was also a part of my life outside school which was quite secure and healthy.

However, I was frightened of how to actually deal with it, how to reveal it. My self-confidence and self-esteem were so badly affected that I began to doubt myself. Do they mean that I am mental, weird, queer? My sensitivity may have aggravated it. Maybe it was like an invisible magnet, because over-sensitivity can impair your judgement of what is a joke and what isn't. I was cornered, trapped. I was so distressed, traumatised, hurt that I was rendered literally speechless about what was happening to me. I felt wounded. I used to cry and cry on my own at home and even on holidays. It felt like somebody was beating down on my heart with a hammer.

Coping with that kind of hurt is terrible. I was in my late twenties when I finally sat down and wrote out what had happened. My only way of communicating it was by writing it.

I think the whole spontaneous, natural element of your personality is crushed by bullying. Your responses/reactions to all kinds of things in life are not natural any more. They have become injured, so your natural enthusiasm, enjoyment and happiness in things goes. It's like being numbed. You become guarded, suspicious. You begin watching other people. You watch yourself. You don't know how to be relaxed with people. You become fearful of opening up, fearful of further rejection.

Bullies are also adversely affected by their behaviour. My research in schools showed that they were absent most often and left school at the earliest possible opportunity in greater numbers than other students. Bullying is only one of a range of disruptive behaviours engaged in. Bullies are often in conflict with the school authorities. Other studies have shown that people who bully at school are more likely to be involved in criminal activity in adult life and are less likely to have a full-time job or a successful marriage.

Bullies and their victims suffer long-term effects as a result of this behaviour. Both groups need help.

PART III

Responses to Bullying

Introduction

'Parents care about their own children. The biggest challenge facing me is getting them to care about other people's children.'

    School Principal, prior to a talk for parents on bullying

Individuals, organised groups, even government departments are challenging bullying behaviour worldwide in response to the growing awareness of the consequences of such behaviour. The challenge facing all of us is the co-ordination of these varied responses to send out a simple but clear message, 'Bullying is not acceptable'. A community approach to bullying is, I suggest, the optimum way to achieve this goal.

Developments in various countries

Norway

As already stated, two young people took their own lives in late 1982, and it emerged that longstanding victimisation was the reason for both these tragic incidents of suicide. Arising from this, the bullying problems were discussed at the top level of the Ministry of Education. At the prompting of the Minister of Education, a working party was set up. It was decided that a nationwide campaign against bullying in primary and secondary schools should be conducted, starting on 1st October 1983. The campaign was aimed at teachers, parents and pupils. A video film about bullying, and written material for teachers and parents, were distributed to all 3,500 primary and secondary schools in Norway. The Ministry of Education provided the finance for this. Professor Dan Olweus was given responsibility for examining how serious the problem of bullying was. This was to be done by means of a questionnaire, the analysis of which would represent a nationwide sample of schools. The Ministry of Education provided funds for a follow-up project, which was called the Janus Project, to investigate the effect of the Campaign Against Bullying of 1983.

The very organised, scientific approach to countering bullying has been very successful in raising public awareness of the issue. In addition, there has been a reduction in the incidence of bullying in schools which have introduced active policies to deal with the behaviour. Given the extensive nature of the approach it will also be possible to chart changes over time. It should be stated that this comprehensive approach would have been impossible without extensive financial support from the Ministry of Education.

Japan

Because bullying interferes with a person's education, it is taken very seriously in Japan. The National Police Agency has actually drawn up a definition of bullying (*ijime*) which goes as follows:

> Attacks on a particular individual, physical and/or through the force of words, involving threats or pushing, shoving or punching, being shunned by their classmates, psychological pressure continually repeated, resulting in suffering to the victim.

Greenlees, in an article in *The Times Educational Supplement* (2.4.93), entitled 'Harsh regime blamed for bullies,' refers to figures from the Ministry of Education's national register which showed that 22,100 bullying incidents were logged at state-run schools during the 1991-1992 academic year. In response to this, the Health and Welfare Ministry appointed 14,000 welfare officers to work in schools. All of the appointees had experience of dealing with children. The new welfare officers formed a national committee to monitor the situation in schools and serve as a link between home, school and the education authorities.

On the 20th May 1994, a Tokyo court decided that city authorities were partly responsible for the suicide of a student who had been harassed and ridiculed in a mock funeral at school. The ruling was the first to hold school and local authorities responsible for dealing with bullying. It was ordered that compensation should be paid to the parents of the dead boy.

England

In England, there has been reaction to bullying behaviour on a national level. Michele Elliott, a child psychologist and director of Kidscape, a charity against child abuse, studied some 4,000 pupils. Government guidelines based on Elliott's research have been published in a 150 page guide and sent to Britain's 35,000 state schools. The following extract from the Kidscape booklet, *Stop Bullying*, gives a good description of the research:

Bullying – Pilot Study

From 1984 to 1986 Michelle Elliott conducted a pilot study on children's safety. 4,000 children, aged 5 to 16, took part and were asked about their worries and concerns. Children talked about everything from getting lost to being frightened by bad dreams and the prospect of a stranger taking them away to certain death. One surprising aspect of the study was the overwhelming problem of bullying. 2,720 of the children (68%) complained of being bullied at some time. Most of these incidents occurred when travelling to or from school or in school. The children reported that they were usually bullied when no adult was present.

These children were then asked in more detail about their experiences. 1,520 (38%) of them had been bullied more than once or had experienced a particularly terrifying incident. Of the 1,520 children who were bullied more seriously, 1033 were boys (68% of the victims) and 483 (32% of the victims). 121 of the boy victims (8%) and 63 of the girl victims (4%) seemed to be chronically and severely bullied to the point that it was affecting their everyday lives. Some of these children were terrified of going to school, were often truant, ill or had attempted suicide.

The reported bullies were mainly boys – 80%. 20% of the reported bullies were girls. The vast majority of the bullies were at least one year older than their victims; most were even older – 2 years or more.

The parents of the children in the pilot study were also asked about their concerns for their children. In addition to the concerns about abuse and the issues mentioned above, the parents expressed anxiety about bullying. Approximately 30% considered bullying to be a threat to their children. The most common advice given by them to their children was to fight back if bullied. Very few of the parents had tried any intervention to stop the bullying (4%), preferring rather to 'let the kids settle it'.

The Gulbenkian Foundation is a charitable trust. In recent years, through its education programme, it has sought to address the problem of bullying in schools. The starting point was to try and raise awareness of the prevalence of bullying, its damaging effects on children, and to convey to schools that specific measures could be adopted to reduce it. To this end, it funded the publication of a range of advisory material for teachers, governors and parents.

In 1989, the Foundation set up an advisory working group on 'Bullying in Schools'. It has supported the development of a survey service for schools by Yvette Ahmad and Peter Smith. This enables schools to carry out a survey and to receive in return a folder of information on the extent of bully/victim problems in their school, in which classes it is located, where it happens and what form it takes.

Hull, in the North of England, has been the scene of a most interesting community-based anti–bullying project. The area targeted (North Hall/Orchard Park Estates) has about 3,000 children. The area has a very high rate of unemployment and various other social problems associated with economic disadvantage. The project seeks not only to reduce the kinds of community, school and workplace hostility/aggression known as bullying but also to prevent the circumstances from which such tendencies develop in young children and become more refined as they grow older. Voluntary and statutory agencies, community representatives and parents all work together to build a community-based anti-bullying campaign. The project is concerned with bullying within both adult and child populations. It works closely with the parents of pre-school children, providing free 'parenting packs' and workshops in order to create positive social skills and good learning habits. This approach is also extended to develop school based strategies to counter bullying. The organisers of the campaign realised that the media could play a very significant role within the community by generating discussion and raising awareness of the issue of bullying. In order to make the campaign accessible to all, posters on the theme 'Stamp out Bullying' were placed in local pubs and supermarkets, giving a confidential telephone number. All families and individuals within the designated area have access to a counselling and intervention service. The project was financed by Humberside County Council and the Hull Safe Cities Project.

In September 1994, Education Secretary, Gillian Shephard, launched an initiative to counter bullying in schools. Every school in England and Wales will receive anti-bullying videos and leaflets. Ministers want to help school heads by creating a new climate of understanding and sympathy in schools.

Scotland
In Scotland, Andrew Mellor, an experienced teacher, carried out research into bullying in ten secondary schools, commencing in October 1988. As a follow-up to this research, the Scottish Office Education Department (SOED) commissioned the Scottish Council for Research in Education (SCRE) to produce a pack which would assist schools in developing policies against bullying. This was published in 1992 with the title 'Action Against Bullying'. It was distributed to all Scottish schools and subsequently to schools in England, Wales and Northern Ireland. To date, well in excess of 40,000 copies have been distributed. The success of the first pack led to the development of a

second pack. This focuses on ways to involve families and non-teaching staff. It was published in September 1993 with the title 'Supporting Schools against Bullying'. Such was the interest generated by the two packs that the SOED agreed to fund a service which would be based at SCRE with Andrew Mellor acting as Scottish Anti-Bullying Development Officer. His brief is to work with education authorities and schools which are developing their own initiatives to counter bullying, and to carry out school-based studies with the aim of producing support materials.

A further interesting initiative occurred in June 1993, when Tayside Regional Council appointed a bullying/truancy team, consisting of three full-time development officers. The team is available to all schools in the region to help them draw up and implement anti-bullying policies. In March 1994, a telephone helpline was launched, offering a free confidential counselling service to any child or young person in Tayside region who is experiencing problems with bullying. The line functions Monday-Friday, 3-9pm. At the same time an anti-bullying parent helpline was established, staffed by the three members of the anti-bullying initiative with the back–up of the Education Support Service. The line functions three afternoons per week – Monday/Wednesday/Friday from 2-5pm.

In September 1994, the SOED distributed copies of a leaflet entitled *Let's Stop Bullying – Advice for young people* to all schools.

Ireland
The Department of Education 'Guidelines For Countering Bullying Behaviour in Primary and Post-Primary Schools.'
At the end of March 1993 the Education Minister announced the setting up of an expert working group to draw up guidelines for countering bullying behaviour in schools. The draft guidelines were completed by early July and teachers, unions, parents and school management groups were consulted and their recommendations included in

the final guidelines which were released on September 30 1993.

The introduction emphasised 'that the issue of bullying behaviour be placed in general community context to ensure the co-operation of all local agencies in dealing appropriately with it'. It points out that 'Bullying behaviour affects everyone in the classroom, in the school community and, ultimately, in the wider community'.

Bullying is defined as 'Repeated aggression, verbal, psychological or physical, conducted by an individual or a group against others'. Attention is drawn to the fact that isolated incidents of aggressive behaviour, which should not be condoned, can scarcely be described as bullying. The behaviour is bullying when it is systematic and ongoing. Nine different types of bullying are described in relation to pupil behaviour.

In an attempt to prevent bullying, the guidelines recommended 'a school policy which includes specific measures to deal with bullying behaviour within the framework of an overall school code of behaviour and discipline'. Co-operation and consultation are emphasised. 'The managerial authority of each school in developing its policy to counter bullying behaviour must formulate the policy in co-operation with the school staff, both teaching and non-teaching, under the leadership of the Principal, and in consultation with parents and pupils. In this way, the exercise of agreeing what is meant by bullying and the resultant development of school–based strategies for dealing with it are shared by all concerned.'

In raising the awareness of bullying in its school community, so that they are more alert to its harmful effects, schools could choose to have a staff day on the subject of bullying, complemented by an awareness day for pupils and parents/guardians.

Within the school there should be definite procedures for

dealing with incidents of bullying behaviour. Parents/ guardians must also be informed of the appropriate person to whom they can make enquiries regarding incidents of bullying behaviour which they might suspect or that have come to their attention through their children or other parents/guardians.

The non-teaching staff should be encouraged to report any incidents of bullying behaviour to the appropriate member of staff. Serious complaints should be reported to the Principal or Vice-Principal who could impose the appropriate disciplinary sanctions and make contact with the parents if necessary.

The guidelines say that pupils involved in bullying behaviour need assistance on an ongoing basis. In conclusion, the guidelines refer to the desirability of the inclusion of a module on bullying behaviour in the pre-service training of teachers, which would be a positive step in alerting potential teachers to problems caused by such behaviour in schools. Also, it considered that the expansion of in-service courses to teachers on aspects of bullying behaviour would be of considerable benefit to the teaching profession in the process of raising awareness and developing techniques to deal with such behaviour.

When the Minister for Education launched the guidelines, she committed herself to establishing a psychological service to cover the whole primary sector and an expansion on the *Stay Safe Programme* to the post-primary sector. From January 1994, she promised a major expansion of training for teachers and part of this initiative will include a module on countering bullying behaviour in schools.

The Stay Safe Programme
The *Stay Safe Programme* is a teaching package, designed for primary schools. It aims to prevent child abuse by equipping parents and teachers with the knowledge and skills necessary to protect children in their care. Children are then taught safety skills in the normal classroom con-

text and these skills are reinforced through discussion with their parents. This approach increases community awareness and makes children less vulnerable to abuse of all kinds. The programme was developed and researched by the Child Abuse Prevention Programme and is the result of a two-year pilot study.

The programme was designed on the basis of consultation with teachers assigned to the project by the INTO, and ongoing discussions with the Departments of Health and Education. It consists of a video for children, two separate curricula for junior and senior cycles, a training course for teachers and an educational component for parents.

The programme, which is now being made available to schools nationwide, contains a chapter on bullying and a lesson component for work with the pupils. During the piloting of the *Stay Safe Programme*, it became clear that bullying was an issue of major concern to teachers and parents, and that there was need to tackle the problem in a structured way.

The section on bullying points out that 'children who are victims of bullying often feel shame, guilt or a sense of failure because they cannot cope with the bully. It is important that parents don't pass on a sense of disappointment in the child's inability to cope. They should acknowledge bullying as a problem that everybody comes across at some stage (and place the guilt firmly with the bully)'. The rules of the *Stay Safe Programme* seem particularly appropriate when dealing with bullying: 'Say "No", Get away, tell and keep telling.'

Childline
Childline is a service provided by the Irish Society for the Prevention of Cruelty to Children. It is intended for any child in trouble or danger. By dialing 1-800-666-666 any child anywhere in the country can talk to a voluntary counsellor about anything they wish. The service is non-directional and nonjudgemental and children can approach

anonymously. Childline takes no action unless a child empowers it to do so. When a child asks for help, whatever their problem, the option of going to a trusted adult within their own community or being referred to an appropriate agency is discussed with them. Since the service was launched in 1988, it has received more than 277,000 calls. In 1992, there were 551 counselled calls on bullying. In 1993, this had risen to 1,080, a 96% increase. The chief executive of the ISPCC, has stressed the need to get away from the adult attitude that it was 'part of growing up – it did us no harm'. He points to an IMS survey which found that 36% of people said they had been bullied as children, and 17% had done the bullying.

The ISPCC also worked with Kidscape (UK), the Department of Education and the National Parents Council (post primary) in the production of 'Stop Bullying', a set of guidelines for use by parents and teachers in an effort to prevent, identify and respond to the problem of bullying.

Discipline in the primary school:
Report of a survey incorporating aspects of bullying in school.
In November 1993, the Irish National Teachers Organisation (INTO) published this report. It is the result of a nationwide survey on the question of discipline in schools, which was conducted in May 1993. Chapter five refers to bullying and comments on the incidence of bullying in primary schools, analyses some of the causes for it, and examines some of the courses of action which are being used at present to combat it.

The survey analyses the results for 452 schools, including various types of school (large, medium and small; boys, girls and mixed schools) in urban, suburban, rural and inner city areas, and in the various standards in primary schools. 57% of schools had a policy on dealing with bullying but 77% felt that bullying is becoming a more acute problem. The highest increase in the incidence of bullying appeared to be in the third and fourth classes. Name calling was found to be the most common form of bullying. 99% of teachers were of the opinion that bullying occurred in the school yard. In order to improve the situation, the report raises the possibility of parents assisting with yard supervision but draws attention to the legal minefield with regard to responsibility. Increasing supervision by teachers would cause a deterioration in teachers' conditions of service and would therefore be impractical. 78% of teachers felt that children had to contend with bullying on the way to and from school.

The INTO survey gives valuable information about bullying in schools from the teacher's perspective. It illustrates clearly that it is incorrect to look only for a school based solution. The survey contends that bullying is caused by a combination of psychological and domestic factors. The school has a role to play as part of a broad based approach supported by society in general. I fully endorse that view.

What parents can do

Bullying is a secret activity. Most people do not tell others directly that they are being bullied. However, there are certain things to watch out for. One on its own is probably not important, but a combination of the following may be:

* Physical signs. Children may experience persistent headaches and upset tummies. Bed-wetting may occur. Some children may have scratches and bruises and be unable or unwilling to explain them satisfactorily.

* Attitude change. A child who has been very happy at school or in a club seeming to lose interest – not putting the same effort into homework. Over a period of time there may be a very definite drop in academic performance. Some pupils may also drop out of sports and other favoured activities which they have taken part in after or outside school.

* Mood changes. These occur most often when a child is

about to return to school after a break. This would be most obvious after a long break such as summer or even Christmas and Easter holidays. However, even at a week-end the change can be seen. On Friday evening, Saturday all day, and Sunday morning, the child is happy and occupied. However, on Sunday afternoon and evening, the child may be on their own much more, appear preoccupied and tense. Any mention of school may cause irritability. Going through their mind may be the following questions: 'Will that person be in tomorrow?' 'Will I go to the yard?' 'Will I go to school tomorrow?'

Children may also be persistently in bad humour on coming in from school each day. Having eaten, they should be in better form. If they are not, and if they seem to take out their bad humour on younger brothers and sisters, something is upsetting them. Some children may become very concerned about their appearance – how big or small they are, the size of their nose or ears, their hair. I am not referring to the normal level of interest which most young people take in this area but rather where it becomes an obsession, accompanied by high levels of anxiety.

* Damage to, or loss of property. Younger children often have a particular liking for certain pencils, rulers and rubbers. Sometimes, these may be broken or hidden. With older children, books may be written in, torn or even stolen. Clothes can sometimes be the focus of attention – ink repeatedly on the backs of shirts and jumpers. Bags may also be damaged. If a student uses a bicycle this may be interfered with.

Occasionally there may be a demand for money or sweets – 'Fifty pence tomorrow or else'. The 'or else' doesn't usually mean that you are beaten up. Comments about how poor you are are just as effective in making children pay up. Sometimes actual lunches are demanded.

* The journey to and from school may be a problem. A child who has walked in and out no longer wishes to do

so. They may ask for lifts – 'Dad, when you're going into work, could you drop me off at school?' A child may say to the mother, 'Mam, will you be doing the shopping around the time school ends? I could meet you.' Sometimes the problem may be happening on the school bus. Quite suddenly, some children may refuse to travel on the bus without good reason.

* Bullying on the road can cause a child to stay indoors a lot. It is most obvious in summer when you expect children to be out playing. Children in this situation usually find that it starts with exclusion from games. It may then progress to verbal or even physical intimidation. If they do go out they may be stalked. One of the most upsetting aspects is when insulting graffiti appear on walls in the local area. Eventually, the child may lose confidence and refuse to go out. As mentioned previously, sometimes entire families are subjected to this kind of treatment. There is usually a ringleader.

If you know your child is being bullied:

* The first thing to do is to assure the child that the problem lies with the bully and not with them. This has the effect of removing the guilt many people feel when they are bullied.

* Detailed and persistent interrogation usually makes the child feel worse. Once they know that they can speak to you, they usually will.

* Both parents should actively support the child.

* Dealing with the problem should be a co-operative exercise between both parents, the child and the school/club where appropriate.

* Parents need to be careful not to give the impression that this is a very minor problem and that they have easy answers. To a child being bullied it is a problem of major proportions.

* If the bullying has been serious, the school should be approached in a low key way, either by letter or telephone. An appointment can be made to speak to the class/form teacher or the principal as necessary. Confidentiality needs to be guaranteed at all times.

* A written record of incidents should be kept with date, time, people and brief details.

* In the past, advice on how to deal with bullying was at two extremes, either to ignore it or to retaliate (either physically or verbally). Neither of these usually works. Assertiveness, which is the halfway position, is the best option. In my opinion, persistent name-calling is a form of bullying. I remember meeting a girl in fifth class in a primary school who had been called 'pig face' for about six months. I asked her how she felt when they called her that and she said 'I feel that I am about an inch high'. For too long we have dismissed name-calling as a bit of fun. Telling a child to ignore name-calling usually does not work, because it shows all over their face that they have heard it. When children are called names, they should literally stand their ground and look the person/persons in the eye. Eventually, they may be able to say 'I heard that and I don't like it'. Parents can help by getting the child to practise looking in the mirror and imagining they are confronting the bullies. Eye contact and positive body language (head and shoulders up) are important aspects of being assertive.

Retaliation in the case of physical bullying can be a dangerous option because it can give the bully an opportunity to say they were acting in self defence. Secondly, if it is unsuccessful it can make a person more vulnerable to physical bullying in the future as they have shown the bully they are physically inferior. Thirdly, this kind of physical exchange can provide a lot of 'fun' for other class members.

* A child who has high self-esteem is most unlikely to be the victim of long-term bullying. Parents can help to build

up self-esteem through encouragement, making them feel good about their appearance and getting them involved in activities inside and outside school. Any activity which leads to a sense of achievement will build up self-esteem, whether it is playing football, a musical instrument or taking photographs.

Some parents wonder if there is a place for martial arts and self defence classes for shy sensitive children. If the motive is the same as for any activity, i.e. to improve confidence and make friends, then such activities can have a very positive effect. However, if they are seen as a means of getting back at a bully or becoming more aggressive, they are not to be recommended.

* I have spoken to many children who have been bullied and who have lost the confidence to reach out to people and make friends. Sometimes I ask 'When did you last have your lunch with somebody?' 'When did you last talk to someone in the school yard?' 'When did you last walk to school with someone?' The reply often is, 'I can't remember.' When pushed a little, it may emerge that it was six weeks ago or even longer. This situation is sometimes complicated by the fact that, among younger children especially, there are changes within groups, so that the former 'best' friend is no longer so. Children must learn to cope with these changes and not allow them to affect their confidence. This also happens in neighbourhood settings. Some children become over-dependent on their parents and look to them for all the answers to any problems they may have. In most cases, at least part of the answer is in their own hands.

* Sometimes a child may be over-sensitive. They need to learn to distinguish between the kind of treatment almost everybody is being subjected to from time to time, and behaviour where there is a deliberate intention to hurt.

A Community Approach to Bullying

The diagram overleaf summarises the main facets of a community approach to bullying. Awareness is a key component and is crucial in the various settings referred to. Parents, schools and clubs should not presume that children and young people know how to behave. It is necessary to make them aware of the effects of bullying. Too often, the excuse is 'We were only messing' or 'We never knew she was getting so upset'. From an early age, parents should discuss with their children the notion of the rights of others, difference and tolerance of differences. Parents should watch out for bullying tendencies in their own children. Within their own neighbourhoods, whether it be a suburban street, a small town or a rural area, people should support one another in standing up to bullying behaviour. The popular view that the bully (whether it be an individual or a family) is a coward is usually true. That is why there is such strength in group disapproval of bullying.

Raising awareness
Within schools, awareness can be raised by means of a staff seminar on the issue, in conjunction with a parents' meeting. Some schools hold a bullying awareness day or week. It may be part of the process of developing a school policy, or where there is a policy, it may become an annual event. In primary schools, especially, the children may be invited to produce posters, paintings and poems on the subject of bullying. These are then displayed prominently over a period of time. Such material can also be used in conjunction with the drawing up of individual class charters. Each class, with the help of their teacher would draw up their own code of behaviour, in their own words. It would of course refer to other issues as well as bullying and should be in a position where everybody could see it every day. The *Stay Safe Programme* has been very successful in raising children's awareness of bullying.

Schools which are in the process of developing a policy

A Community Approach to Bullying

FAMILY

- Awareness
- Parents as role models
- Values

NEIGHBOURHOOD

- Co-operation and support

SCHOOL

Caring ethos

- Awareness
  - Staff seminar. Parent Meeting
  - Anonymous questionnaires for students
  - Bullying awareness day/week
- Policy
  - Emphasis on prevention
  - Whole school approach
  - Teachers, non-teaching staff, bus drivers
  - Anti-bullying code/ Class charters
  - Procedure for reporting and investigating
  - Curriculum
  - Stay Safe Programme
  - Drama
  - Support and counselling (Peer and teacher)
- Reactive Approaches
  - Low key approach in investigating
  - Combination of various strategies

  - Sanctions

WORKPLACE

- Awareness
- Policy
- Designated individual in the personnel department
- Trade Unions
- Sanctions

COMMUNITY PROJECTS

YOUTH/SPORT CLUBS

- Standards of behaviour
- Policy
  - Emphasis on prevention
  - Procedures
- Sanctions

GARDA / POLICE

- Available to various groups
- Preventative role
- Junior Liaison Community Guard/Policeman
- Sanctions

G.Ps (General Practitioners)

often find it useful to assess the student perception of bullying. This can be done very successfully by means of anonymous questionnaires. However, I stress that they must be anonymous. Questions could relate to which year the student is in, how often they have been bullied over a period of time, where bullying happens and whether or not they report it. The school then is in a better position to draw up a policy to suit its particular needs.

Anti-Bullying Code

One of the cornerstones of any policy to counteract bullying is an anti-bullying code. This applies to schools, youth and sports clubs. The advantage of an anti-bullying code is that it sends a clear message to parents, students and members of the youth or sports club that this behaviour is not tolerated. When something is written down it has far more impact than an oral statement. It also removes the opportunity for people to say that they never knew the matter was taken so seriously. The anti-bullying code should be the result of a consultative process between teachers, students and parents or club leaders, club members and parents. In the case of a school, it seems appropriate that the school rules or code of discipline should contain an item referring to bullying behaviour. In a club situation, the anti-bullying code should be clearly displayed in the club premises and if the parents receive a description of how the club is run and what standards are expected, the anti-bullying code should be included.

The following code could be used in a school or club:

In our school/club, everybody is valued. Difference of any type – race, religion, appearance, personality, background or interests – does not make it acceptable to bully a person. We are all different – that's what makes us special. The people in this school/club have the right to be *themselves*, and the responsibility to treat others as they would like to be treated. Silence allows people to suffer. We speak out when we know we should.

Much of what I have written about raising awareness and formulating an active policy for dealing with bullying in schools and clubs could be applied to a work setting. The vast majority of companies do not have a policy. There is very little open discussion of the issue. It reminds me of the way things were in the majority of schools five years ago. The lead could be taken by personnel departments and trade unions.

With the emphasis on prevention of bullying, many schools have made use of peer support programmes and drama in recent times.

Peer Support Programmes
If we, the seniors were instructed on how to prevent bullying, we could at least be of some use to younger years who might feel more confident with an older boy than a teacher.

18 year old boy

Much of the research into bullying behaviour indicates that many of those being bullied do not tell anybody. It is probably easier to tell a friend or your parents than it is to tell a teacher.

Telling a teacher brings with it the risk of being called a 'grass'. In addition, if a bully finds out they may seek retribution. To help overcome these difficulties a number of peer support/peer counselling programmes have been developed.

Buddying is a technique described in the 'That's Life' anti-bullying information pack. Older children are trained to counsel and befriend pupils who are being bullied or are in need of a friend. The use of buddying/bully boxes can enable children to ask for help in confidence.

Peer Counselling
In the London borough of Camden, Acland Burghley School has started a system of peer counselling on the issue of bullying under the direction of Ms Maggie Bentley, the Deputy Head and Ms Lee Saunders, an educational social

worker who was involved in training the students (reported in a BBC TV Programme, Spring 1994). All students from second year up were asked to complete an application form if interested. In the knowledge that an initiative like this carried certain risks and even dangers, the participating students were given very definite direction. They were told that they could not promise total confidentiality, because depending on what was disclosed, it might be necessary to refer the person on to someone else. Their role was to help people with problems about bullying and nothing else. They were told that they were not expected to have all the answers, and often just the opportunity to talk to them and unburden, was going to make a difference for many students.

When the student counsellors had been selected, a display was set up with their photographs and some biographical details. They were given a room in which to meet clients. They were given the title: The Anti-Bullying Counselling Service. Appointments were only available for lunchtime. A rota of counsellors was set up. Each week a meeting of the student counsellors was held, presided over by the Deputy Head and the educational social worker. Students described the cases they had dealt with, focussing on difficulties and options presented to clients. A general discussion followed and was a major source of support for the students. With the permission of the person being bullied, the student counsellors sometimes called the people alleged to be bullying to talk to them. This was probably far less threatening than if a teacher did this. In some cases the two parties were brought together to discuss the situation, usually with very positive results. Simon, one of the student counsellors gave his appraisal of the approach as follows:

> Ms Bentley's decision to open this scheme for pupils by pupils was a very big move and I applaud her for that, because the amount of power we have been given by a group of teachers, who are usually seen to be above

you, was a very brave decision but it was probably the only way that a scheme like this could run.

Meitheal

In Ireland a youth programme called 'Meitheal' has been developed in the diocese of Kildare and Leighlin. In the Irish language the word *Meitheal* refers to the old rural practice of groups of farmers coming together as a community to work on an individual farm at harvest time. In schools, Meitheal is about gathering a group of ten senior students who will work to create a more caring environment in the school. To run the Meitheal programme, there must be full support from the school authorities. It is necessary to find a teacher who sits with the group as a supportive adult who will advise about the workings of the school and inform the staff of the work of Meitheal. It seems to me that this function could be carried out very successfully by the career guidance teacher (if there is one). The programme is launched by a person from Teach Bríde (the organising body) who explains the programme to all students. Students are invited to apply for the programme on a specific form. Each student is interviewed.

Parents of students chosen to participate are invited to the school on a set evening to meet the teacher facilitator. The teacher explains the aims of the programme and tells the parents individually why their son or daughter was chosen. During the summer holidays the groups from each school go to Teach Bríde for a residential training course (usually Thursday to Sunday).

A Meitheal group has a committee drawn from their own members – a permanent Chairperson, a secretary and a P.R.O. who change position from term to term. The P.R.O. communicates to fellow students information about actions the group undertakes. Meitheal works on the basic idea that everyone is special and unique. Over the years, the most successful and appreciated action of the Meitheal group has been in helping first years and trying to counteract bullying in the school. Throughout the year the Chairpersons from the various schools go to Teach Bríde on the last Friday of every month for a meeting with the Meitheal co-ordinator. At present sixteen schools are participating in the programme. The system is now used in other parts of the country.

The use of drama
   It's the first year story
   the one we all know
   It's going to happen to you
   So don't try to act slow
   We're going to start at the top
   and find you the fool
   It's the age-old tradition of every school
   I'm the top number one
   I'm cool-hand Sid
   And have my hand in the pocket of every kid
   I want money, smokes, your CDs too
   You find a new way to go to the loo
   Who's this? – say we don't know
   Who's this? – let the teardrops flow
   Who's this? – he don't smell too good
   Who's this? – he'd get up if he could
   Why it's pig-face
   Mr Pig-face
   Going to have some fun
   Sir Pig-face
   My little pig-face
   We're going to sing your song
   Oink! Oink!
   Mr Pig-face

Drama allows for the expression of feelings and emotions. Often children and adults find it difficult to confront difficult issues. Bullying falls into this category. Drama distances the spectators from the painful reality. It can give them the confidence to discuss aspects of an issue in an impersonal, non-threatening way.

In England, the Neti–Neti theatre company devised a play about bullying called 'Only Playing, Miss'. It was aimed at school audiences of first to third years, but can also play to general and adult theatre audiences. Francis Gobey, the Education Officer for the company, describes the intention of the company: 'With black, Asian and deaf performers playing substantially positive roles, "Only Playing, Miss" implicitly challenges those racist and ablist attitudes which bullies often exploit.' He contends that this approach is particularly appropriate because bullying often has its roots in the fear of difference. The play uses all the resources of drama to breach the silence which bullying relies on. The company offers two kinds of workshop. The first is a series of preparatory sessions on bullying independent of the play. The second type is that which follows the play and involves everyone who has seen it – actors, students, teachers. (See *Bullying ...*, by Elliott, chapter 13.)

In January 1993, the medium of drama was used to counter bullying in an exciting initiative in the Newry/ Banbridge area. Seventeen schools united in a cross-community programme. Pupils from the schools jointly devised a play on bullying which was produced by local teacher, Sean Hollywood. The play was then performed in the various schools, with great success. In Our Lady's Grammar School it led to an advice leaflet for parents and the creation of a Sixth Form Friendship Group, with two sixth-formers being allocated to each of the junior classes, with a brief to befriend, support and prevent or stop any bullying behaviour. On a broader scale, a consequence of the inter-school co-operation in making the play a reality was that it created a netwrok of contacts between teachers, so that in the event of cross-community or inter-school bullying incidents being discovered, people knew who to contact.

In October 1994, the Sticks and Stones Theatre Company began a programme aimed at raising teachers' and children's awareness of bullying and at helping schools to cope more effectively with the problem. The project is funded by the Gulbenkian Foundation and is limited initially to primary schools in the Dublin area. The project centres on a performance of the play in schools, followed by workshops and seminars for pupils, parents and teachers. The project has a full–time facilitator and a research companent.

Role playing is a further aspect of drama which teachers may use to raise awareness of bullying. Like drama, it has the advantage of being nonjudgemental. Children also tend to be relaxed with it because it is a medium which is used to address many issues, not just bullying.

Reinforcing Bullying Behaviour
People in authority, whether in school, club or workplace may instigate or reinforce bullying behaviour. A section from the Department of Education's guidelines seems appropriate in this context. They recommend that the following should be avoided:

- Using sarcasm or other insulting or demeaning form of language when addressing pupils; making negative comments about a pupil's appearance or background;

- Humiliating directly or indirectly a pupil who is particularly academically weak or outstanding, or vulnerable in other ways;

- Using any gesture or expression of a threatening or intimidatory nature, or any form of degrading physical contact or exercise;

To pupils could be added club members and employees. In the workplace people are sometimes humiliated by being asked to do menial tasks, given unclear instructions and then criticised unfairly for failing to complete the job satisfactorily. Their competence may be questioned publicly without reason. It should also be pointed out that, on occasion, figures of authority, be it a school principal, teacher, club leader or manager in the workplace, may be subjected to bullying.

Reactive Strategies

Low key approach

In my experience a low key approach is the most effective way of investigating incidents of bullying.

When an incident of bullying is being investigated, the last thing that the victim wants is a public discussion of their problem. This can be very humiliating for the victim and gives the bully a further audience. A teacher, club leader or member of personnel must at all times assure a victim of confidentiality and only take action with the permission of the victim. In less serious cases, they may just need someone to listen to them. They may then ask for advice. Sometimes the plight of a victim is made worse because either a parent, teacher, friend or workmate has presumed that they had the answer. Dealing with bullying is a delicate matter and the vulnerability of the victim must always be taken into account.

Bullying Incident Form

There should be a recognised procedure for reporting and investigating incidents of bullying whether it be in school, club or workplace. It is a good idea if particular individuals develop an expertise in dealing with bullying. People involved in bullying may avoid having to face up to the consequences of their behaviour because much of the evidence is hearsay. Unless a written record is kept of serious incidents of bullying, it is very difficult to act confidently and efficiently in dealing with the matter. The best way to keep a written record is by using a bullying incident form. Such a form should be uncomplicated. It should have a record of the date, time, place, names of people involved and brief details of the incident. The form should be available to all teachers or club leaders. When such a form is used over a period of time, it usually emerges that the same names are appearing again and again, even though different teachers/club leaders have come across the incidents. The forms should be kept on file and treated as confidential information. They should be stored in a secure place and should be available only to the appropriate persons. These written records are most useful should parents need to be contacted in either a school or club situation. In cases of serious bullying in post primary schools, boards of management may find this information very important in deciding what course of action to take.

Dealing with an incident

Should a teacher or a club leader discover an incident of bullying, the following procedure is recommended:

1. Speak separately to the person alleged to be bullying, the person who appears to be the victim and somebody not directly involved but who saw what happened. It can be useful to get the various people to write down their account of what happened. This is best done in private.

2. Decide which strategy to use. The next section outlines the various approaches.

3. If the teacher/club leader considers the incident to be serious, details should be written down on a bullying incident form. Very serious cases should be reported to the school principal/club leader as appropriate.

4. The principal/club leader should make contact with parents if necessary.

5. The victim of bullying needs to be assured of on-going support and encouraged to report immediately any further attempts at intimidation.

6. Both bullies and victims may need counselling. In primary schools it falls to individual class teachers to do this. Because of the nature of the job and pressure on time, it must be done informally in most cases, at break or lunch time or after school. In post-primary schools, the task is usually carried out by form tutors on a voluntary basis. More serious cases can be referred to the career guidance teacher. The danger here is that if there are too many referrals, the counsellor/careers guidance teacher is unable to cope because of pressures of other work.

In the workplace, the personnel department may be able to provide counselling. Youth Clubs should also consider encouraging one of their leaders to take training in counselling skills.

Strategies

The No Blame Approach, The Common Concern Method, Bully Courts, and Non Violent Conflict Resolution are some ways of responding to bullying.

The No Blame Approach

George Robinson and Barbara Maines, an educ-ational psychologist, have developed an approach to bullying called the 'No Blame Approach'. More than one hundred schools have adopted this approach which, by encouraging offenders to empathise with victims and using group counselling, claims a 95% success rate. There are seven steps in the 'No Blame' approach. The victim is interviewed about who was involved in the bullying and how she/he feels when bullied. Their feelings can be expressed in writing or drawing. The next five steps require the teacher to meet with the people involved (including bystanders or colluders) explaining the problem, sharing responsibility and asking the group for ideas. The optimum size for this group is six to eight and it does not include the victim. Responsibility for solving the problem is left with the group. After about a week the teacher meets each student individually, including the victim, to discuss how things have been going. The main strength of the approach is that it makes it less likely that a bully will seek retribution from a victim for 'telling'. The approach is not above criticism.

Robinson and Maines consider that feelings of retribution towards the bully should be set aside, as the aim is not justice or morality, but to change behaviour and thus achieve the best outcome for the victim.

The Common Concern Method

Gang slagging is the worst. I became overloaded with the weight of peer-induced torment. I still vividly remember the hurt it caused me many times. I often despaired of school which at the time was all my life was about. It has given me, in the long run, a cynical view of life.

18 year old boy

The main features of this approach are:

* It is only used where a group is involved in bullying.

* Group bullying is called mobbing.

* The therapist has individual talks with the suspected mobbers – 10-20 minutes for each talk. After this the therapist speaks to the victim. The parents are not involved.

* About a week later the talks are repeated. Once again this may be on an individual basis. However, they could be spoken to as a group, with or without the victim, depending on the circumstances.

* The success of the therapist (who could be a teacher or a psychologist) is largely determined by the level of empathy which they can express for the sufferings of the victim. Eventually, it is to be hoped that the mobbers will share this sense of empathy. This is the basis of the Common Concern Method.

A more detailed account of this method can be found in chapter 8 of *Bullying – An International Perspective*, edited by Roland and Munthe. The chapter is written by Professor Anatol Pikas of Uppsala University, who devised the approach.

Bully Courts

The charity Kidscape pioneered the idea of bully courts. They started with thirty pilot schools, both primary and secondary. Careful monitoring of eight schools over a three-month period indicated that the courts had been a major factor in reducing bullying. Michele Elliott, director of Kidscape, emphasises that the bully courts will only work in schools which have a strong anti-bullying policy which is supported by parents, teachers, staff and children. The court should be seen as the final link in the chain of a complete anti-bullying strategy.

Under this system the students elect two representatives and the teachers nominate two more. A teacher acts as adviser. Parents should be invited to a meeting to see a mock court in operation. Students need to agree guidelines for behaviour and to sign contracts. The guidelines are then displayed prominently throughout the school. The court would meet once a week at a set time. The verdict would be binding on all parties with a right of appeal.

Non Violent Conflict Resolution (Walker, 1989)
The essence of this approach is that the use of violence in any form, be it on the personal, social or political level, is condemned. The objective is to resolve the conflict so that all sides have their own needs met, at least partially. The concept of a 'co-operative' classroom is central. In this kind of classroom, the groundwork for non-violent conflict resolution is laid. (See *Bullying* ... Roland and Munthe (eds), chapter 11.)

Any person using the approaches listed above is advised to study them carefully and decide (a) if the approch is suitable for their circumstances at all, or (b) what modifications need to be made to render it appropriate. In the vast majority of cases, I find that any approach is best set in an overall low key framework.

Sanctions

At a certain point it may be necessary for a school, club or workplace to apply sanctions. These should be part of the overall policy. Unless action is taken in serious cases, bullying behaviour is encouraged. Unchecked bullying can lead to absenteeism and underachievement at school, drop out from clubs or requests for transfers to different departments in certain companies. In very severe cases some employees may have no choice but to leave the company altogether. In schools and clubs persistent bullying can be tackled by contact with parents and suspension if necessary. Some schools and clubs use a system of withdrawal of privileges or ask those involved in bullying to sign a contract of good behaviour. In clubs, it may ultimately be necessary to ask certain members to leave. In the workplace, personnel departments should ensure that the pressure is on the person bullying to change and not on a victim to leave in order to escape this negative attention.

The role of the Garda (Police) in countering bullying

In dealing with bullying behaviour, the emphasis of the Garda Síochána is on a preventative approach. Over 600 gardaí have received special training and are involved in a schools' programme for primary schools. Junior liaison officers are being trained to deal with the problem in post-primary schools. As well as bullying, the schools' programme deals with vandalism, road safety and the investigation of crime. The involvement of the gardaí is very much in line with the recommendation of the Department of Education guidelines that the problem of bullying behaviour is best tackled using a whole community approach involving parents, teachers, non-teaching staff, social and community workers and the gardaí where appropriate.

There is no offence listed as bullying and the gardaí have no direct legal powers in dealing with it. However, if there is an assault, formal action can then be taken. In certain situations a breach of the peace could be interpreted as an offence. In the case of a person demanding money this could be a form of larceny. It is the intention of the gardaí to deal with juvenile offences outside the court system if possible. In instances of bullying, the gardaí carry out their investigations in a very discreet manner, with the emphasis on trying to get the bully to change behaviour sooner rather than later.

Doctors

Finally, doctors may discover from time to time that bullying may be the cause of symptoms such as headaches and stomach problems among children. In the absence of all other causes, it may be appropriate to raise the possibility of anxiety at school, to which bullying may or may not be a contributory factor.

Helping Bullies

I'm a pretty big person and fairly clever. How do I pick out who is a dick? Certain things annoy me and so do people.

14 year old boy

I have described earlier how the victim of bullying can be helped. However, those who bully also need help. The quotation above implies a very antagonistic attitude. Many people who bully have a very positive attitude to aggression. This isn't always expressed in physical terms. People bully for different reasons, but the root cause is linked to a sense of power. Some bullies are victims themselves in other situations and attempt to compensate for this by picking on somebody weaker and more vulnerable than they are. Others enjoy the sense of power their behaviour gives them. In a sense, their behaviour is gratuitous. It is my firm conviction that the most effective strategy in helping bullies is to develop an ethos which does not tolerate bullying behaviour, whether it be at home, in school, club or workplace.

Occasionally, however, some people will bully irrespective of the ethos of the school, club or place of employment. The first step is to make the person aware of the fact that their behaviour is unacceptable and causing distress. It is important to find out why a person is bullying. It could be that personal difficulties at home are the cause of the problem. In some work situations, those in a managerial position feel under pressure themselves to improve the performance of their department. Anxiety may cause them to bully others. A good personnel officer can do much to prevent these situations escalating. In schools or clubs a particular individual could be encouraged to develop expertise in dealing with bullying behaviour. Most second level schools also have the advantage of having a career guidance teacher who may be able to do a certain amount of counselling. A very small number may have a teacher who specialises in home-school links. Many people engaged in bullying respond very positively to somebody who listens to their story nonjudgementally.

It is worrying that there is so little back-up in terms of a psychological service available to help in very serious cases of bullying. In primary schools it falls to the individual teachers and principals to deal with the very severe cases of bullying. In a situation where the main cause of the behaviour lies outside the schools, there is a very limited amount the school can do. Social workers may, however, have a role to play.

The Theory in Practice

The preceding section of this book has described in some detail ways of preventing and dealing with bullying. In order to implement this, I suggest that there is need for an exploratory meeting between various parties on the issue of bullying. This applies equally in schools, clubs and the workplace. It is encouraging to report that this preliminary stage has already taken place in many cases. It is necessary that somebody in authority organises such a meeting.

In the school situation, the principal is the key person. He/she is in a position to involve others in countering bullying. The exploratory meeting could ideally include representatives from the Board of Management of the school, the teaching staff, the Parents' Association, the senior students, the non-teaching staff, the bus company and the community guard. Such a meeting could be the springboard for drawing up an active policy to counter bullying. It would be a whole school approach in the real sense of the term.

In the workplace, the lead could probably be taken by the personnel department. The meeting should include representatives from employees, management and the trade unions. Finally, in clubs, the club leaders could convene a meeting between themselves, parents' representatives and senior club members.

In all three contexts, a meeting like this is the opportunity to begin to act to prevent bullying rather than wait for it to occur, and then decide what to do.

Conclusion

Like lots of problems in life, people really only become aware of bullying when they are directly affected by it. The stress and suffering of many men, women and children exposed to bullying was the impetus for writing this book. For too long bullying has been considered to be a problem which occurs only in schools. It was often accepted as part of the process of growing up and was even believed to have had a beneficial effect in that it toughened people up and prepared them for the 'real world'. However, bullying affects people of all ages and goes on in all walks of life. Because of bullying, some people fail to reach their potential in school or even leave early. Others are forced to leave their jobs and some may even have to move house. Bullying may destroy a person's confidence and lead to a lack of trust in and suspicion of others. In some cases it may be the root cause of depression. Ironically, some people who are bullied may go on to bully others, because they were never given alternative strategies to counter the behaviour. Those who bully are less likely to enjoy successful relationships. They are more likely to be involved in criminal activity.

Bullying happens because it is allowed to happen. It is

wrong to presume that children know how to behave. From the earliest possible age, parents and teachers need to raise awareness of what bullying is, the effects that it can have, and how on occasion we can actually be involved in bullying without being aware of it. Parents have the opportunity to do this in an informal way. Schools need a more structured approach. Caring for others underpins the fight against bullying. The issues of tolerance and tolerance thresholds must be considered, because when tolerance levels are low, the weak and the vulnerable suffer. Victims of bullying do not inflict pain on others, yet they are not allowed to be themselves. Some of them may lack certain social skills and even irritate others but that can never justify the treatment they are subjected to. Lecturing young people about the evils of bullying does not generally work. The aim should be to sensitise people to the sufferings of others and work on feelings of empathy by using drama, peer support programmes and day to day teaching opportunities. In this way the unacceptability of bullying is not something that is highlighted once or twice a year at assembly or when a serious incident happens, but becomes part of the school ethos.

In schools, the workplace, youth and sports clubs, there is a need to increase awareness of the anti-social nature of bullying behaviour. There should be a far greater focus on preventative measures. The approach should be pro-active rather than reactive. The aim should be to move away from responding to individual incidents of bullying to creating an atmosphere where they are less likely to happen in the first place. There is a need to break the cycle at an early stage.

When bullying occurs, victims do want something done about it. However, it must always be on their terms. I recommend a low key approach.

In Ireland, the Department of Education has provided guidelines for countering bullying behaviour in primary and post-primary schools. They need to be supported by resources for a full psychological service for all schools, in service training for all teachers on the issue, and funding for scientific research.

Bullying is an abuse of power whether in the home, school or workplace. It is the responsibility of each individual and each community to stand up against it. Bullying weakens the very foundation of a civilised society.

Resources

In the last few years a large number of books, packs and videos on bullying has been produced. Below I list some of the most useful ones.

Books and Reports

Adams, Andrea, *Bullying at Work, How to confront and overcome it*, Virago, 1992.

Besag, Valerie, E., *Bullies and Victims in Schools: A guide to understanding and management*, Open University Press, 1989.

Byrne, Brendan, *Coping With Bullying in Schools*, The Columba Press, Dublin, 1993.

DFE Sheffield Bullying Project Report, University of Sheffield, 1993. Available from: Project Director, Professor K Smith, Department of Psychology, PO Box 603, University of Sheffield, Sheffield, S120 2UR.

Discipline in the Primary School: Report of a survey incorporating aspects of bullying in school (1993), Irish National Teachers' Organisation (INTO). Available from: INTO, 35 Parnell Square, Dublin 1.

Michele Elliott, ed, *Bullying – A Practical Guide to Coping for Schools*, Longman, 1991. A collection of articles covering all aspects of bullying, and suggesting strategies for reacting and coping with bullying in schools. Available from: Longman Group, PO Box 88, Fourth Avenue, Harlow, Essex, CM19 5SR.

Guidelines on Countering Bullying Behaviour in Primary and Post–Primary Schools (1993), Department of Education, Dublin. Available from: Government Supplies Agency, Publications Branch, 4/5 Harcourt Street, Dublin 2.

Kidscape, *Stop Bullying*, Kidscape/ISPCC/National Parents' Council (post–primary), 1993. Available from: ISPCC, 20 Molesworth Street, Dublin 2.

Mellor, Andrew, *Bullying and How to Fight it: A guide for families*, Children who are bullied often feel frightened and powerless and their families feel angry and frustrated and uncertain of what to do. This booklet provides practical advice on how families can tackle the problem. Toppics covered include: spotting danger signs; getting advice; helping victims; contacting the school; good school practice and last resort action. Available from SCRE, 15 John Street, Edinburgh, EH8 8JR.

Olweus, Dan, *Aggression in the Schools: Bullies and Whipping Boys*, Hemisphere, 1978.

Olweus, Dan, *Bullying at School: What We Know and What We Can Do*, Blackwell Press, 1993.

Roland Erlling and Elaine Munthe, eds, *Bullying: An International Perspective*, 1989, Trentham Books Ltd., 734 London Road, Oakhill, Stoke–on–Trent, ST4 5NP

Skinner, Alison, *Bullying: An Annotated Bibliography of Literature and Resources, 1992*, Youth Work Press, National Youth Agency, 17-23 Albion Street, Leicester, LE1 6GD.

Tattum, Delwyn P. and Lane, David A, eds, *Bullying in Schools, 1989*, Trentham Books Ltd., Unit 13/14 Trent Trading Park, Botteslow Street, Hanley, Stoke–on–Trent, ST1 3LY.

Tattum, D. P. and Herbert, G.,, *Bullying: A Positive Response, 1990*, A booklet which examines the dynamics of bullying and the elements needed for a successful anti-bullying campaign. Primarily geared to parents, governors and staff in schools. Available from: Cardiff Institute of Higher Education, also Scottish Consultative Council on the Curriculum,

Information and Marketing Services, Gardyne Road, Broughty Ferry, Dundee, DD5 1NY.

Tattum, Delwyn and Herbert, Graham, *Countering Bullying: Initiatives by school and local authorities*, Trentham Books, 1993.

Packs

We Don't Have Bullies Here, by Valerie E Besag. Comprehensive pack of materials from which any school, college or youth group can develop their own policies, practices and staff training programmes. Contains an overview of the problem, examples of preventive work, response strategies, whole-school approaches, ideas for videos, and workshops addressing specific issues.
Available from: V.E. Besag, 57 Manor House Road, Jesmond, Newcastle Upon Tyne, NE2 2LY.

A Positive Approach to Bullying: a workshop for professionals involved with children/young people from nursery to further education, Eve Brock 1992. Training pack that provides a one-day workshop in which teachers and other professionals involved with children and young people can look at the issue of bullying, and how the school/college/youth group can take a positive, pro-active approach towards it. The materials include: guidelines for the facilitator; discussion and exercise handouts; case studies; and resource and contacts lists. Available from: Longman Group, PO Box 88, Fourth Avenue, Harlow, Essex, CM19 5SR.

Action Against Bullying: A Support Pack for Schools by M Johhstone, P Munn and L Edwards, 1992. Consists of a booklet and support materials for use in school staff development and policy action groups. The materials offer a range of practical ideas and approaches for individual teachers and schools. The booklet is divided into two main sections: 'Identifying Bullying, Bullies and Victims' and

'Anti-Bullying Action', while the support materials include: action on policy papers to help plan, develop and publicise a practical anti-bullying policy; scenarios; discussion starters illustrating different types of bullying; and a listing of curriculum materials and ideas for in-service work. Available from: Book Sales, SCRE, 15 St John Street, Edinburgh EH8 8JR.

Supporting Schools Against Bullying: (1993) Scottish Council for Research in Education. Anti-bullying pack that focuses on involving everyone in an anti- bullying action strategy. The pack contains two booklets, the booklet for families by Andrew Mellor and 'School Action Against Bullying: involving parents and non-teaching staff', which provides guidelines for head teachers on involving the whole-school community in the school's anti-bullying policy. Available from: Book Sales, SCRE, 15 St John Street, Edinburgh, EH8 8JR.

Handbooks and Videos

The No Blame Approach by Barbara Maines and George Robinson, 1992. Video and support workbook that has been developed from a successful, thought-provoking school-based programme to deal with bullying. It asks staff to question existing practice and challenge the idea that support for victims or punishment of bullies will prevent future incidents. The video introduces a step by step, teacher-led initiative which enables them to intervene effectively when bullying occurs. It encourages other pupils to become part of the solution and hopes that those who are bullying will express helpful attitudes and change their behaviour, encouraged by not being punished. Available from: Lame Duck Publishing, 10 South Terrace, Redland, Bristol, BS6 6TG.

Promoting Positive Relationships: Bully Proofing Our School by Alan McLean, (1992) aims to provide a framework and process to enable schools to analyse and manage the problem of bullying. It advocates a whole-school approach and a joint partnership among pupils, parents and teachers. The pack includes a training programme for teachers, parents and senior pupils, workshops and curriculum programmes (primary, secondary and special schools), practical ideas for the playground and guidelines for assessing problems and self–reporting survey questionaires. Available from: Alan McLean, Strathclyde Region Education Department, Clyde House, 170 Kilbourne Road, Clydebank, Glasgow, G81.

Sticks and Stones
For 11-16 year olds, parents and teachers produced by External Affairs, Central Television, Broad Street, Birmingham, B1 2JP.

Bullying In Schools
This video summarises research into bullying, carried out in Australia and elsewhere. It is intended to raise awareness and to promote discussion amongst parents, teachers and senior students. Case studies of an individual bullying incident and the development of a whole policy are included. A small booklet accompanies this video.

Available from: Australian Council for Educational Research, Radford House, 9 Frederick Street, Hawthorn, Victoria 3122, Australia.

Contacts

Irish Based Contacts

Please note that not all the organisations and telephone help lines in this section are solely (or primarily) concerned with bullying.

Organisations

* National Parents' Council (Primary Tier)

Hogan House, Hogan Place, Grand Canal Street, Dublin 2. Tel: 01/6613022

* National Parents' Council (Post–primary Tier)

Contact: Ms Ruth Brenock, Curraband, Ballinacurra, Midelton, Co Cork. Tel: 021/631369

* Campaign Against Bullying

Contact: Ms Vivette O'Donnell, 72 Lakelands Avenue, Kilmacud, Stillorgan, Co Dublin. Tel: 01/2887976

* Waterford Bullying Awareness Group

Contact: Ms Bernadette Lambe c/o St Brigid's Family & Community Centre, 37 Lower Yellow Road, Waterford. Tel: 051/75261

* National Association of Parents

Contact: Mr Tony Egan, 'Massabielle', Athlone Road, Ferbane, Co Offaly. Tel: 0902/54245

* Parentline

Carmichael Centre for Voluntary Groups, North Brunswick Street, Dublin 7. Tel: 01/8733500

* ISPCC

20 Molesworth Street, Dublin 1. Tel: 01/6794944

* Barnardo's National Children's Resource Centre,

Christchurch Square, Dublin 8. Tel: 01/530355

* Mental Health Association of Ireland

Mensana House, 6 Adelaide Street, Dun Laoghaire, Co Dublin. Tel: 01/2841166

Telephone Help Lines

* ISPCC Tel: 01/6794944

* Childline Tel: 1800-666-666 (children only).

* Samaritans (see local directory for number).

* National Association of Parents. Tel: 0502/20598

British Based Contacts

Organisations

* Anti–Bullying Campaign (provides advice and a referral service for parents and children, victims and bullies), 44 Priory Drive, Reigate, Surrey, Reigate, RH2 8AR.

* Scottish Council for Research in Education (provides advice to local authorities, schools and parent groups). Contact: Mr Andrew Mellor, 15 St John Street, Edinburgh, EH8 8JR.

* Kidscape (provides advice for parents, teachers and children), Contact: Ms Michele Elliott, 152 Buckingham Palace Road, London, SW1W 9TR. Tel: 0044/71/3599392

* Children's Legal Centre (provides free and confidential advice service), 20 Compton Terrace, London, N1 2UN. Tel: 0044/71/3599392 (2-5pm)

* Scottish Child Law Centre (provides legal advice for parents and children), 170 Hope Street, Glasgow, G2 2TU, Scotland. Tel: 0044/41/3339405

* Parentline, Westbury House, 57 Hart Road, Thundersley, Essex, SS7 3PD, England. National Office Tel: 0044/268/757077

* Childline, Freepost 1111, London, N1 OBR, England.

Telephone Help Lines

* Childline Tel: 0044/0800/1111

* Children's Legal Centre Advice Line Tel: 0044/71/3596251 (2-5pm)

* Advisory Centre for Education Advice Line Tel: 0044/71/35488321 (2-5pm)

* Scottish Child Law Centre Tel: 0044/0800/317500 (freephone advice line for under 18s)

* Anti–Bullying Campaign Tel: 0044/71/3781446

Index

Anti-bullying code 67
Assertiveness 63
Atmosphere in school or club 22
Awareness 65-66

Body language 24-25, 63
Bullies:
    Definition 20
    Descriptions of 12-13
    Helping 80-81
    Risk factors 20-24
Bullying:
    Definition 20
    Descriptions of 10-11, 13-14, 18-20
    Dealing with an incident 62-63, 75
    Effects of 13-15, 42-47, 82
    Incident form 74-75
    Modelling of 23
    Neighbourhood 31-32
    Numbers involved 20
    Reinforcing 73
    Sports clubs 34
    In the workplace 28-30
    In youth settings 32-34
Bully courts 77-78
Bully victims 24

Childline 58-59
Common Concern Method 77
Counselling 75-76

Confidentiality 63
Conspiracy of silence 41-42

Difference 22-23, 25-26
Doctors 80
Drama 71-73

Fear 38

Garda (Police) 79-80
Gulbenkian Foundation 53, 72

'In' Group 16
Initiation rites 37-38
INTO Report on Discipline 59-60

Jealousy 23-24

Kidscape 52-53

Low key approach 37, 40, 63, 74, 83

Name-calling 11, 14, 59-60, 63
No Blame Approach 76
North Hull Anti-Bullying Project 53-54

Parents:
    Signs to watch for 60-62
    What to do 62-64
Peer Support Programmes:
    Buddying 68
    peer-counselling 68-70
    Meitheal 70-71
Provocative victims 22

Responses to bullying:
    England 52-54
    Ireland 55-60
    Japan 51
    Norway 50-51
    Scotland 54-55
Retaliation 39-40, 63

Sanctions 78-79

School buses 35-37
Self-confidence 16, 39
Sensitivity 21, 64, 83
Shame 38-39
Silent majority 15, 41
Slagging 11, 13-14, 16
Stay Safe Programme 57-58
Strategies 76-80

Telling tales 38

Victims:
    Descriptions 11-12
    Definition 20
    Indications 39
    Risk factors 20-24
    Not telling 38-40